Early Praise

This deceptively unassuming book is actually a considerable accomplishment, along the lines of V.S. Naipaul's *A Way in the World*: a sequence of seemingly disparate essays that, together, form a beautiful and powerful narrative of self-knowledge.—David Shields, author, *Reality Hunger: A Manifesto*

We forget to remember that what we think of now as "creative" nonfiction has not been around for, like, forever. David Hamilton (let's call him the self-effacing founding father of the self) was there from the startling start, there for the endowing of all the alienating effects, the defamiliarizing of the newly weaponized ordnance of "ordinary" life. A dandy documentary, *A Certain Arc*, is a kind of fossil record of those revolutionary moments, but it is also a defining demonstration of the form itself—mesmerizing memoirs, murmurations, essay after essay—ecstatic, elegant, elemental, enchanting. Here is profound husbandry, restorative curation. Here are the articles of our confederation, our articulating articulation of our nascent art, our enabling apparatus of our unconventional convening.—Michael Martone author of *Brooding and The Moon Over Wapakoneta*

As one would expect from such a distinguished educator and editor, the prose in this collection is beautifully turned, the intelligence luminous, and the experience and wisdom of a lifetime generously shared: this book is a gift to all literature-lovers. But what seems even more striking and rare, in this age of self–absorbed memoir, is the curiosity and openness of its author, his worldly willingness to learn from others–in short, his humility, which is the true mark of an ethically refined sensibility.—Phillip Lopate, author, A Mother's Tale

Like the map in the kitchen of his childhood farmhouse, David Hamilton's remarkable essays chart intersecting rivers of time, exploring swirling depths of self and nation, strong currents of love and friendship, and the adventurous waters of his literary calling as a celebrated writer, teacher and editor. An extraordinary, inspiring journey!—John T. Price, author of *Man Killed by Pheasant and Other Kinships*

In settings ranging from the small-town Missouri of his youth, to rural regions of Colombia and Gabon, to his office as editor of *The Iowa Review*, David Hamilton shows again that he is a brilliant and consummate essayist. Ghosts animate these pieces—which is fitting, given the retrospective nature of memoir—as do colleagues, poets, autofictionists, family, and people he meets on the road. More than just a miscellany, the essays are linked in surprising ways—on video night in Gabon, for instance, who appears on the screen but a high school classmate leading a famous jazz band, a classmate who had suggested, when they were kids, that David might do better if he wasn't so self-conscious; of course, being in Gabon makes him painfully self-conscious, as does meeting Hunter S. Thompson in Colombia, as do his first years as a professor. Throughout, a large heart takes in the world, and gives it back to us with wisdom.—Tom Lutz, author, *The Monkey Learned Nothing: Dispatches from a Life in Transit,* founder and editor in chief of the *Los Angeles Review of Books*

Whether reading about Hamilton's racial awakening as a white child in small-town America, or his behind the scenes anecdotes as long-time editor of the venerable *Iowa Review*, or his sometimes perplexing conversations with Gabonians while overseas visiting his daughter, you'll gently wade into each piece at once comforted by the soothing, lyric prose, only to soon find yourself in the deep-end of the heart and mind. This is a masterclass in the art of the essay.—Jerald Walker, author, *The World in Flames: A Black Boyhood in a White Supremacist Doomsday Cult*

David Hamilton is the very definition of literary citizenship. These essays on his life and labors in the service of letters are as rich and storied as they are humble and instructive. From Iowa to Gabon to Barranquilla, you'll share in his ongoing anticipation and joy of discovery. Reading *A Certain Arc: Essays of Finding My Way* is like stumbling upon a cachet of seasoned love letters—each one elegantly penned, daringly intimate, and, amazingly, still perfumed.—Marc Nieson, author, *Schoolhouse*

As a fellow longtime literary editor this collection rings especially true to me. Hamilton's experiences and his writing remind me of why I love literature.—Speer Morgan, editor *Missouri Review*, author, *The Freshour Cylinders*

Poet, memoirist, and editor for three decades of *The Iowa Review*, Hamilton weaves digressive threads into unified tapestries. He writes about race, gender, and social justice as preoccupations; and about our cultural and personal histories during his lived life. He is above all a genial, earth-bound intellectual, lover of reading and writing well, and of the natural world.—DeWitt Henry, author of *Sweet Marjoram: Notes and Essays*

David Hamilton might seem to be a late bloomer, but in fact he has been blooming for many years. His lantern was long hidden under the bushel of *The Iowa Review*, which he edited. It turns out that he was, all along, a writer of extraordinary perception and poise. His account of his days (32 years) at The Review give the best picture I know of the charms and delights—and terrors—of being a devoted servant to writers. He was always a country boy of the most exquisite taste and sophistication. Aw shucks, I exclaim, what a nice guy, and, boy, can he write.—Howard Junker, founding editor of *ZYZZYVA*

A Certain Arc

Essays of Finding My Way

David Hamilton

Ice Cube Press, LLC (Est. 1991)
North Liberty, Iowa, USA

A Certain Arc: Essays of Finding My Way

Copyright © 2019 David Hamilton

First Edition

ISBN 9781948509077

Library of Congress Control Number: 2019933950

Ice Cube Press, LLC (Est. 1991)
North Liberty, Iowa 52317
www.icecubepress.com | steve@icecubepress.com

The paper used in this publication meets the minimum requirements of the American National Standard for Information Sciences—Permanence of Paper for Printed Library Materials, ANSI Z39.48-1992.

Manufactured in USA

Cover drawings and author image by Rebecca Clouse

for Rebecca, Jenny, Colin,

and in memory of Toni

Contents

Prelude

"By the time you are grown and aging," said a Haida elder on public radio, "you need to have a tale, your life should have been a life that permits a tale. Why should anyone care about you later if you have no tale to tell?"

Hometown

My hometown spreads from the intersection of two U.S. highways. It has a courthouse and a square. The courthouse features a soaring dome over a square tower with clocks on all four sides and light bulbs outlining the dome's four curving ridges. Except during the energy crisis of the seventies, that courthouse has been a landmark from afar. Even now when approaching after a long absence, I strain before I'm quite conscious of it and seek my first glimpse of a lighted dome rising above the trees. As a boy, riding into town with my parents, usually standing behind the front seats with my brother, and especially after dark, we vied to see it first. Had I read Fitzgerald by then, I might have thought of its glittering yellow outline as a festival tent hovering above our maples and elms. Now two sets of grain elevators rise into the same sky, disturbing, without erasing, a book mark in my memories.

When rivers led settlers inland, a much smaller town fourteen miles north had seemed to promise more growth, but railroads reversed all that, leaving Marshall, toward the center of the county, the landlocked focus. The square marks its center, and the two highways approximately quarter the whole. Each quadrant has its grade school—Northwest, Southeast, Benton, and Eastwood—deflections from consistency, being, I suppose, a virtue.

Three of the four grade schools economized on the same architectural design: a U of hallway, with classrooms arranged along its outer side, embracing a small auditorium and gym. Our high school was essentially two grade schools stacked. Its U was longer and broader, with more classrooms opening off it, and the auditorium contained a balcony, a stage, and a full-sized basketball court; but its shape was the same. Northwest, the eccentric, two-story grade school, was the town's original school.

We lived in a two-story frame house with attic, basement, and a wrap-around porch, with front steps on the right side of the porch, if you faced it, and a cement walk that divided four mature elms, two on either side of the walk as it led to the street. Houses to the left and right, across from us, and up and down the street were similar, as if advertisements for Middle America, with generous front yards and fountain-elms that arched over Eastwood all the way to Lincoln, a half mile west, then to Brunswick, about a quarter mile farther, leaving half a quarter more to the grade school named for the street on which it stood. To the east of us, Eastwood became U.S. 240, running out of town, curving north, straightening, dipping across Salt Fork Creek—the old bridge not two lanes wide and bumpy enough to slow an incoming car or truck—then turning sharply north before rising to Montague Hill, making two more quick turns, north then east to Slater, Glasgow, Moberly, and across the Mississippi to Chicago and New York if you persist. Or, as a highway west, Eastwood leads past our grade school and on for another couple of blocks before the road jogs north by the train station, left past the grain elevators and Northwest School before streaming out of town toward Malta Bend, Kansas City, Denver, and San Francisco.

That much mapping and more was fixed for me by our "breakfast nook," just off the kitchen, where we ate most of our meals, the walls of which my parents had papered with maps from *National Geographic*. All around us countries spread out, cities and seas, quite a few of those names changed by now, and my brother George and I would challenge each other to find Luxembourg, or Thailand, or Libreville, the capital of Gabon. It's not that our parents were world travelers. Missouri and Illinois pretty much defined their territory, with forays into Michigan, Wisconsin, and the Boundary Waters of the Quetico-Superior canoe country just off the northern border of Minnesota. Later they would make it to Alaska, England, France and take an African safari, but that was after George and I had grown and left home. Meanwhile we cast our eyes outward, and though I was hardly overwhelmed with wanderlust urges, we both took to geography at school, reinforced as those lessons were by our almost daily, mealtime game. "I'll bet you can't find the capital of Ethiopia," one of us might say and could hardly finish saying before the other had jumped up to point out landlocked Addis Ababa.

Often enough another game absorbed me as I sat on the curb in the summer dusk with Wayne, Charlie, and Albert, watching for and, since Albert was legally blind, listening to cars and trucks wind down as they topped that last rise before settling onto Eastwood. Our game was to identify their make and year; "Forty-seven Ford, Forty-nine Chevy," one of us would sing out, often Albert with a sureness that astonished me. We are given our gifts, or find our way to them, by giving ourselves to what calls us, which at that age was motor song if you were Albert, Charlie, or Wayne.

Charlie and Wayne lived across the street from Albert and me, with their back yard running down into woodland, to a ribbon of creek, along which, in stones smoothed over ages, we identified the "Indian Bathtubs," before climbing uphill to Yerby, half a mile south of us, and to another set of boys whom we barely knew until we met them in high school. Every so often there were skirmishes, more often rumors of skirmish—the BB-gun wars—around the bathtubs between Sammy, Danny, and Ben and their friends and ourselves.

Carolie, a year younger than I, lived a few doors west on Eastwood. We had one afternoon together in her attic—those hot, still attics of summer—rummaging through old clothes; trying things on being our way of revealing something of ourselves. An image of her in white panties comes to me now, her bare chest very like my own although we each had glimmerings of the much that would come of difference we did not fully uncover, a difference that would send me repeatedly into an old, abandoned swimming pool in an otherwise empty lot to the side of her house that afforded cover for my staring at her well lighted, upstairs window. But the angle was not in my favor and Carolie had been schooled by then to pull her shades.

My brother and I made pocket money mowing lawns, raking leaves, and shoveling snow season by season. Once George started a fire in leaves he'd raked up for neighbors, and that caused a stir and no doubt some restriction that I no longer remember. But chores and small jobs were the smaller part of it. The hours I spent throwing a ball against the front steps then fielding it as it caromed onto the lawn—with rules I'd devised to distinguish an out, single, double, triple, or home run—shooting baskets on the back of our garage, or driving a tennis ball just over the net line painted waist high beneath the basket were not quickly overcome by those I have since spent writing and rewriting paragraphs, though I expect by now I've succeeded in doing that much.

We'd stream out of Eastwood School with that last bell in May to have day after day before us, whole days to play and to improvise our playing, much of it solitary, or "self-employed," like my cat who is off to work outdoors after breakfast every morning. But often, too, after supper we'd run back outside for hide and seek, kick the can, one game after another played into the dark, or just to linger among friends until our parents called us home, my father by a whistle famous throughout the neighborhood, using both index and middle fingers to shape his tongue for a wheet, whuuu, wheeeee, long-short-long, that reached deep into any backyard. It seemed it would be a different lifetime when we were called back to school.

On long afternoons on the porch, I pored over newspaper stories of war, the terrifying pornography of soldiers executed in the snow, with bullets to the back of their heads, along a roadside in Korea. Or, shortly later, the Bobby Greenlease case in which the six year old son of a Cadillac dealer in Kansas City was kidnapped and murdered by a couple of mishaps named Hall and Heady who collected a grand ransom for the time, about one third of what's possible in six figures, but got no farther than St. Louis and then were executed, in short order, and without appeal. I remember reading the even more deliberate pornography of their executions, stripped to their underclothes in the gas chamber, she resisting the fumes as best as she could, he gulping them in.

Running Eastwood, for I often ran my Eastwood mile—the walk sectioned in five foot cement blocks, which I tested by lying down in one and comparing my height—I tried for one stride per block and couldn't quite manage as each step lost a little ground and every so often I stepped on a crack rather than between them. No matter, I flew across Conway, a small street running off to the north, connecting with nothing, but introducing an African American neighborhood with its own Albert, Charlie, and Wayne though I could not yet name a single individual. I saw too that the main floor of the court house on the square had separate drinking fountains marked "Colored" and "White," and once when alone, with all the office doors closed, their opaque glass windows apparently blind, and as my steps echoed under the high ceiling on the cold, tile floor, I sipped from the Colored fountain and found no difference except for the taste of transgression. We knew too that Lincoln School, about the size of Eastwood, lay to the south of us, halfway to Yerby, and served its own population.

More often my path was out the back door, past our garage, across my bare earth basketball court, to enter an old garden lost to grass, with a maple and a Concord grape arbor, to climb over a sagging wire fence and step onto abandoned pasture. My trail angled to the right for a quick dip and another rise into a grove of young Osage orange. Now my back was to the house, which I could see no longer, and my view to the north, with forest in front of me and on my left a peninsula of grassland that leveled off for at least two flights of an arrow. Forest arched around it, from well beyond Carolie's house on my left, all the way over and past Albert's backyard on my right. Leaving that grove, I angled downhill into the woods, to a clearing I favored around a mature oak, then on through forest, by several possible trails that led me, sliding and stumbling downhill, to a creek. The railroad tracks ran beyond the creek bed, but following the creek, keeping to my side of it, I knew several paths that curved back toward Eastwood and could lead me to any number of backyards.

Across the creek and uphill again, just out of sight, was the "Missouri State School for the Epileptic and Feeble-Minded," as was then said, a label both cruel and inaccurate. It had large grounds, including two lakes and imposing brick buildings. It was in fact a kind of prison for the hapless, the hopeless, the forgotten, and abandoned. They were prisoners as much as patients and once in a while one would "escape," putting the whole town on alert, especially Eastwood. More than once one was found on his own idyll along the creek, copping a smoke, watching squirrels run along tree limbs, mild of manner, very likely sedated, passing, like me, an afternoon out of doors.

As a threat, the State School and its patients were modest enough and so my parents seemed to understand, although there must always have been a small chance of a Heady or Hall, who had murdered the Greenlease boy, somewhere among them. To a large extent, it was a sadly comic place that added a small band, always dressed in white, to local parades, a band whose exuberant director would occasionally be a guest musician at church where his specialty was playing "Yankee Doodle" and "Dixie" simultaneously, one with each hand. Occasionally we would go fishing on one of the State School ponds around which some of the inmates also stood, similarly absorbed in the water and its cover for blue gill or bass, and so motionless that it was hard to imagine any of them as dangerous. Still their proximity, the State School grounds being perhaps three quarters of a mile from my back yard as a crow might fly, added to my sense of stealth, as did the possibility of the African American boys following the tracks from Conway into my territory, or a tramp or other wanderer along those tracks from Lord-knows-where, or my brother and his small gang, or any of my neighbors. For I considered all that territory my realm, and it is curious now amid so much memory of shared play in the front and backyards along Eastwood that I think of my behind-Eastwood exploration as solitary. It was a realm of escape, of secret hiding places, a space for time beyond a clock. I never had a watch until after college, when I married. And as for a smart phone, this was 1950 plus or minus; we didn't even have television.

When I crossed the fence from our backyard and slipped into my grove of Osage orange, it was first to flop down, under cover, and take a long view away from home. The bark on the trees was a light, grayish-brown; the spear-shaped leaves had a smooth rounded butt. I could wrap a hand around the trunk of any one of them or grasp two as if climbing some sort of ladder, which in a way I was, to look out over rolling land and down into the woods. In my imagination I was an Indian youth on the brink of being tested or an early French explorer who entered this territory a century before Lewis and Clark. The Osage and Missouri Indians had shared this country for several centuries, and I could imagine myself a member of a hunting party. Robin Hood was another fantasy favorite. Or a soldier on patrol in the Korean War.

We were a farm family, almost. My father and uncle farmed together in the Missouri River bottoms north and west of us. Floods were frequent enough to discourage homebuilding out there, so we lived in town and commuted. A rectangle of land, 433 acres, roughly a mile and a half by half a mile, my father and uncle having cleared most of it, the farm was a patchwork of fields, the Front Field, the New Field, that the most recently cleared, the Middle Field, the House Field, the Long-Narrow Field, and the North Field. There was no house on the House Field, only a pile of rough-milled boards that had once been one. We played on an abandoned combine, left for its value in odd parts. The North Field was heavy with gumbo, and usually, in late summer, dry and cracked; the Front Field was sandy loam. Half circles of timber, with cottonwoods soaring tallest, stood east in the Middle and west in the Long-Narrow Fields. Drainage ditches ran east to west at several places; one of those, bordering the Middle Field, opened on a marsh with cattails, willows, and redwing blackbirds. A dogwood patch rose out of it onto higher ground and curved back into the field. I don't remember any dogwoods, but it was a patch my father and uncle well remembered clearing. Then they left a strip of woods—of "timber," that was the term—about the width of a field, between the Front and New Fields, a reminder to my brother, my two cousins, and me of what the farm had been. Thick with cottonwood, wild plum, mulberry, box elder, and soft maple, it suffered our paths, our hideouts, and our approaches to a raccoon's tree or the fox's den.

Back in town, Eastwood was my terrain. Most grade school mornings, Albert would stop by for me; then we would walk past Carolie's, hoping she would join us. We'd pick Johnny up half a mile along the street. He lived next to Sue, who was by that time usually paired with Carolie. Another quarter mile was Ann's house and less than another the school. The playground to the side of the school featured a ravine with no improvements, just trees, shrubbery, unmowed grass. That's the area we favored during recess more than the ball diamond and jungle gym.

All of us happened to live on and so walked the north side of the street. A few doors past Johnny's, Conway joined Eastwood. Tarred rather than paved, it extended about a block, hooked around to the east, and stopped. We called the African American families who lived there Negroes, politely. But we didn't know their names and hardly recognized faces.

I remember one exception. I had just moved to town and so was seven. I'd come from Illinois and a town with fewer and less visible blacks. In fact one of my earliest memories is holding hands with the one black girl in our first grade class as we joined at recess in some organized game. I remember a vague sense of adventure in either allowing myself or choosing to be paired with her and a feeling of gallantry when I told my mother that evening. She shrugged it off as the small matter it was.

But one afternoon now, sitting along Eastwood with new friends, I called Peggy a n----- —the first and I think only time I've volunteered that word aloud. Peggy, a grown woman, lived with her mother right on Eastwood, an anomaly within the

11

fabric of our neighborhood. I didn't say it to her face; I spoke softly, as she walked past, experimenting no doubt, since I had certainly heard the word spoken by my friends. But Peggy heard me. Wielding a coffeepot, she swung around and chased me across the street, all around Harold Mack's house and deep into his backyard. I was made to apologize, which means she must have spoken to my parents. Only cordial words ever passed between us after that, and once in a while, I would pause and sit on the porch with Peggy and her mother. But I was never invited inside, nor was she, insofar as I can recall, ever a guest in our house.

I grew closer to Reverend Harvey Baker Smith, who also lived only a few doors away. Reverend Smith wore a cutaway when he preached and looked like a cartoon though not comic senator. He was said to have been chaplain to the United States Congress, and he looked the part though I find no confirmation of it. I led the youth group of his church for a time, and he meant to make a minister of me. One summer, when television was new and Dr. Smith had one, I got into the habit of coming around to his house to watch the Friday night fights. It was the era of Rocky Marciano, Jersey Joe Walcott, and Ezzard Charles; and it was disturbing, he said, and wrong, to see a black man and a white man fight.

He used that expression, "black man." I'd never heard it before, and it sounded strange. I sensed its accuracy but was unsure of connotations. I can remember his worried look, as if sparring with divine matters, while he stared hard at the fight and let his ice tea, served by Shelby, his grown daughter, dampen the magazine on the floor beside his couch.

Whatever the year, though, and on most mornings, several black kids would appear from Conway as we made our way to school. They crossed Eastwood and walked up the south side, in separate procession, as we continued on the north. A block before we came to our school, they turned south again and walked another few blocks to theirs. We never spoke to each other as I recall, hardly eyed each other directly. "Dark cloud going south," Uncle Henry would say when passing a few Negroes on a country road. And so that group appeared to us, moving west then south, while our own small cloud, deeply overcast in its own ignorance, paralleled them for the block we shared.

As I grew older, I'd walk Eastwood alone, going or coming home, at dusk or later, and all through high school I'd feel an edge of unease if I passed a black boy, or man, in the dark, though usually he'd be on the south side and I on the north. If I saw him looming ahead on my own sidewalk, I might cross to the other side, affecting an attitude to suggest my real purpose took me there. When I became embarrassed at that poor tactic and held my ground, I steadied myself, brought any humming or whistling to a halt, and controlled my measured pace until we passed. We probably looked at each other, probably nodded. Often I'd break into a run a few steps later, reasoning that I was used to running Eastwood anyway, for practice. In high school I did become an adequate quartermiler. If I saw the stranger from far enough away to make it seem I wasn't running just because of him, I'd pass him flying and keep going, holding my stride steady, one step for each of the five-foot sections of the walk, at least trying to hold it steady until he was well behind me. My shadow pursued me, shortening, as I approached a streetlamp, then leapt ahead, lengthening, as I passed beneath the light.

Summers meant putting up food, canning and freezing. On certain early mornings, my father and uncle and I, with perhaps my brother and cousins, would go to the farm and pick several burlap bags of sweet corn. We'd have a few rows of it growing along the edge of a field, just far enough in not to be obvious from the road, but planted like the other corn, with the field planter. Or sometimes we'd collect field corn if we caught it on the few days when it was sweet and tender. Then we'd return to town where Mom and Aunt Jean would be making their own preparations, tables and tools set out in the backyard, pots of water near boiling. We'd all set to shucking the corn, then slicing it from the cobs. Okra, beans, peas, tomatoes—we put up lots of food—but the corn I remember most. Some we'd can, other batches package for freezing. Mother drove us to the locker we rented downtown, and my brother and I helped her carry the packages into the storage room where we spent several minutes rearranging things in our bins, staying there just long enough, shivering in our T-shirts, to imagine being unable to get out. Then we returned to the best meal of the year, sweet corn and sliced tomatoes, steaming stacks of the one, slices piled high of the other, and as much as we wanted, my mother's face damp but glowing over each platter she brought to the shared table.

Through the winter, my father was usually deep in projects. He worked in our basement, where he had a darkroom and shop. He was a good photographer, and I helped him develop pictures, especially of Indian artifacts. One winter we made a reflecting telescope; we finished grinding a lens he and Mother had begun years before and mounted it so all the neighborhood kids could see the rings of Saturn. Another winter we got some Osage orange staves—the best for making bows—and worked on our own, shaving and shaving it into shape, until, in our quest for elegance, we went too far, and it cracked. Small matter in the long run though because two of his friends, twin brothers in Sedalia, happened to be accomplished craftsmen of bows. They made an Osage longbow for my father and its twin, except for being but half the strength, for me. My bow was about my height, and I loved taking it out onto that back pasture where I launched arrow after arrow into the sky. The arrow would arch up, tearing a hole in air, almost to the edge of sight, then slow noticeably as its force ebbed before leveling off and plunging back to earth. For quite some time I might run after it, find it, and launch it again, my favorite arrows those I had fletched myself, gluing turkey feathers to dowel rods I bought at the lumberyard.

Late one summer, in the season of wild plums, we found a dead raccoon on a gravel road and my father braked sharply, salvaged the animal, and threw the carcass in the back of the pickup, thinking what I needed most was a genuine coonskin cap. We came right home and set to work in the basement, my father turning that old raccoon over on its back, holding the tail in his left hand, slitting the skin along the belly with the knife in his right. The hide must have been tougher than expected, or the knife duller, for Dad had to dig in, get stiff purchase on the knife, and suddenly the tail snapped right in half. "Shit, piss, fuck, cunt," and I drew back, surprised that he, too, knew those words. Even now I can feel their rapid fire and am a little amazed at the unconscious control of assonance and consonance that fixed them in such quick order.

By the second grade and off and on until college, Carolie, the girl from nearly next door, fueled my dreams. Walking past her house brought me to attention, and I was more than tolerant of her younger brother, about the age of mine, simply because of his access to special knowledge. Her parents owned the drive-in restaurant on the northwest edge of town, leaving her at home with her grandmother as they ran it in the evening. Many a summer night, I slipped into the empty pool in the vacant lot beside her house, under the soft light of her window upstairs, its shade always drawn, or at least mostly, for the window glowed like stained glass in my imagination. After a time I'd creep below her window and toss twigs and pebbles against the screen. Carolie'd come and ask, "Who's there," more to be certain than to find out. Then she'd join me on her L-shaped front porch. We'd sit in the swing and talk. We hardly ever touched. Kissing her—clearly the thing to do—was as hard for me as it would have been to cross Eastwood and walk among the blacks, though I was always dreaming of escorting her to one of my places, the lean-to or the wigwam in the woods behind her house. We never had trouble talking; we seemed to know how to say everything except, perhaps, exactly what we felt. Coming close counts for something in love just as it does in horseshoes.

Then her parents would come home. We'd recognize their car gliding down Eastwood and would still the swing while they turned into the drive and continued back to the garage. As soon as they got behind us, Carolie would slip inside and I off the porch. In my memory, the bridal wreath was always in bloom. Soon, though, another car was in her drive and another boy on her porch. For by the time serious dating started, Carolie's friendships ran well beyond our neighborhood, and being pretty, popular, and a destined head cheerleader, she awarded the years that mattered to the first-string quarterback in the class ahead of us, then to the guard with the effortless jump shot in ours.

In the ninth grade, we learned of the Brown decision and that blacks would join us the following year. We still called them Negroes, at least most of us did. Late that spring, our English teacher was protesting that this just wasn't right. The "coloreds and the whites" weren't the same and shouldn't mix. "It would lead to the mongrelization of the species," she said, "and that meant miscegenation"—thus teaching us the word—and no good could come from it. She "wouldn't stand for it," though it wasn't at all clear what else she intended. "God made the races separate," she continued, "and so he meant for them to stay."

That's when Carolie raised her hand. "Maybe God's changed His mind," she offered.

The next year, black kids did filter in among us. Most stayed at their own school or dropped out; they had, as we said benignly, their choice. Some choice. Their own school, after the eighth grade, was thirty miles south, in Sedalia, by bus. That next year, though, Walter and Eugene came off Conway and joined our classes. They didn't walk to school with us; by then, our ways to high school were more varied anyway. When we were on the street together, though, as long as I can remember, they walked the south side and we the north.

There was at least one exception. Carolie, Eugene, and I were walking home one afternoon, perhaps our junior year. Eugene was in my advanced algebra class, where we had gotten to know each other. Clearly this was an experiment. But overtaking us by car, Carolie's mother squelched it: "Carolie, you get in here right this minute." The invitation was not general. Carolie reminded me of that story at our twenty-fifth reunion, after I'd reminded her of her visionary response in that ninth-grade class. We were both telling our stories to Eugene, who was listening patiently and letting us hear him say "black," which was not yet the word when we went to school together.

I was the eldest of four cousins; fieldwork grew incrementally and gently enough for the three of us who were male. We helped with the later stages of clearing, picking up chunks of wood after plows had turned over the new fields in the spring and throwing them in piles for burning. We cut off willow sprouts showing up in the same season to discourage the timber's reclamation of the field. I had my own axe, smaller than full-size, and axe work has always held some romance for me. I learned to aim beneath the soil, where earth, rewoven through winter, allowed a firm, clean cut as it supported the new, subtle shoots. For if I struck too high, the sapling just sprang back and the axe quaked in my arm and hand, stinging like a baseball bat.

Eventually we got to tractors. My father was careful not to work us too hard, not a full day when I started at eleven or twelve. Soon my brother could be held back no longer and we shared a tractor, one of us sitting under a cottonwood with a pocket watch, making sure the other didn't exceed his hour. From such starts, we grew into full days rapidly enough and took pride in driving well—backing tractors up so the hitch pin dropped right in the waiting hole of the wagon's tongue, tripping and lifting the plow out of the ground and dropping it back in after a tight turn right on line for a new furrow. Or by pulling on a lever at my side and braking one wheel, I lifted the cultivators out at the end of the rows, two sets of blades suspended from either side of the tractor, turned tightly but smoothly and dropped the "shoes" as we called them right back in around four new rows of corn without taking out a stalk—for one row nicked meant all four, if you got careless. Soon pesticides turned cultivators into a relic, but the work mattered at the time.

When it came time to drive, I'd driven tractors and a farm jeep enough to feel at ease behind the wheel. I remember riding to the farm with my father and mother one day as I approached sixteen, and Dad pulled over saying, "I guess Dave had better get some practice."

"Can he drive?" Mom inquired.

"I expect so," Dad replied, and I slid behind the wheel and drove off. It was easy, though parallel parking took a few tries later that afternoon. The night after I got my license, my parents let me take the farm jeep out to see friends. One girl told me later how she and her sister and mother had laughed when I came to their house in that funny little car with a motor "that sounded like a sewing machine."

Soon someone always had a car. Whereas my pedestrian knowledge of the town had centered on Eastwood and a few neighboring streets, as far in as the square, cars allowed us to encompass the town in a crisscrossing circuit, and to discover friends who weren't neighbors. After Sunday School, Saturday afternoons, and most evenings of the week, we would be out and around, and much of the time in a car. We dated, or double-dated, more often cruised with friends. The circuit was constant. Up Eastwood, around the square, out to Carolie's drive-in on the northwest side; back to the square and south past the high school, to a second drive-in on the south edge of town; back in toward the square then straight east on Yerby to the city park, spacious and hilly with a curving drive that leads to Eastwood, about a quarter mile from my house, and then back to the square. Probably by now I have written more paragraphs than I made circuits of that town, but I can't guess when writing gained the advantage.

Upstairs, over the shops on the northeast corner of the square, between the courthouse and a church, was our Teenage Club with a snack bar, a room for pool and ping pong tables, and a dance floor with booths set around it and a jukebox. There was no membership policy and no fees. We paid only for candy bars, cokes, and the jukebox. It was open afternoons after school, Saturday and Sunday afternoons, Friday and Saturday nights. Our circuits around town always brought us by the Teenage Club, to its shrewd reconciliation of all that was inevitable within some sense of limits.

We entered through a flapping wooden door off an alley and a parking lot shared with the neighboring church. The door, with no latch, except for a padlock when closed, was the kind you might find on an outhouse. One of the town's two banks faced us right across the street, and the square with the courthouse was catty-corner; we were not on our own exactly. But we could forget to notice. The stairwell, steep, squaring around to the right, gave the sense of an urban tenement—assuming we could imagine one from movies we'd seen—or at least of space alone as in an upstairs room or in an attic. Parents never came up there except for the cherubic mother of one schoolmate who ran the place, and familiarity allowed us to ignore her as easily as we shrugged off town management.

The pool and ping pong rooms opened first off the stairs. Skill at pool, that well-known sign of a misspent youth, was a skill that mattered. If, as my uncle would say about our work on the farm, one boy's a boy, two boys are half a boy, and three boys no boy at all, there, a small crowd at pool was distinctly animal, the symbology so flagrant as to be comic. Girls rarely ventured into that room and never hung around there, though they did move back and forth past us. It was a place for adopting a certain swagger, for holding on to your stick, gesticulating firmly, not shaking but pointing, then chalking your tip. Bending over your shot in that peculiarly rigid right angle, you thrust your blue-jeaned butt out as if it were a fist, the bowed crouch of your legs suggesting what they wished to enclose but had yet to actually embrace. Then the luxurious fondling of the stick, running it back and forth across the notch between your first knuckle and thumb canted upward, or through the teasing circle made of your left thumb and index finger. Back and forth, back and forth, the cue did its slow dance, back to the lip of the notch and forward, unpartnered but advertising. The rigidity in the posture, the tension in the arms, permitted increasing muscle to flex. Then the controlled violence of the stroke, the cue extended and dropped briefly over the felt, the player thrusting himself erect, already in stride for his next shot, the ball rammed home in the pocket. The difference between those who played pool mostly and those who stuck to ping pong, mostly, was the difference between alpha wolf and the rest.

And it was a whole lot easier to carry off the posture there than in the next room where the girls really were and where dancing happened. In there, the edge came off the swagger. We had our alphas and others of dancing as we did of pool, and they didn't line up exactly. Still, some boys, mostly pool players, were there for business, however much they succeeded. They would be the ones, more often than not, leaving with their girlfriends quickly, hustling them off to cars parked in the alley and to the country roads all around us. Others, who played more ping pong than pool, might be there more as friends, hanging out as long as time allowed, then going home quietly and unspent.

We spent hours in that room, dancing less than drifting from one booth to another, talking, talking, even playing solitaire, one version known as "Idiot's Delight," a reduce-the-spread-to-one stack game we could almost play in our sleep and played usually at a booth with friends. One more feint toward connection. All this amounted to delay, of course, while being close to action. We were mostly "Great Pretenders" in that era of the Platters, the years just pre-Elvis; and as he came on the scene we were throbbing. Dancing was fast and separated, barely, as the jitterbug led to the twist; but the slow stuff counted too, less cheek to cheek than breasts to chest, thighs to pelvis, the convolutions of arms and sweaters, your right arm, if you were a guy, reaching all the way around and beginning to brush her right breast, while keeping the irregularities of your erection behind the corset of your Levi's zipper.

Of course, African Americans never joined us, and whether they were told no or whether they never ventured, I cannot say. Integration of the swimming pool was more quickly resolved, democratically and fairly though not without some stalling and boycotting through a first season. But the Teenage Club, with pool and dancing allowed, was out of bounds, and within a few years it folded.

The semi-permanent tease of the Teenage Club makes any remaining sense of off-limits banal and silly. Still, every community has its places within easy reach but oddly denied. We had, for example, the Mary Lou Theater, a firetrap, my parents warned, and on the far side of the square. It featured Saturday afternoon serials. Legend had rats running across the stage and friends hitting them with large red marbles stolen from tin reflectors, a brief fashion over headlights on cars. As it was, there were two safer movie houses, the New Mary Lou and a drive-in on Montague Hill to the east of town. Both prospered modestly while the Old Mary Lou closed.

In its block were the tough bars, where if you walked past, you might stumble into a fistfight crashing out the door. Don't ask me how such rumors started, but I always walked that block cautiously even on a weekday afternoon. Later the football coach, under whom I suffered sufficient embarrassment, renovated a store on that street and I felt slightly ill at ease just stopping by to visit. Later still, coming home with a university friend, we chose one of those bars for a few beers, with my brother, and with a slight spirit of adventure, my brother warning us again as we went inside.

A whorehouse stood near Scudder's junkyard. At least one was said to. Red light and all, though I never saw it. In my eagerness to believe, I reasoned they just stuck the red light out late at night, switching bulbs on the porch. Walking past in daytime, which I seldom had reason to do, I never saw any indication of the place being other than shabby and private. Nor did I ever notice a red light when driving by at night.

Another difficult place was the barbeque joint near Lincoln School where an African American neighborhood spilled down one side of a slope and crawled up another. Driving by, we'd see cars clustered around it, men coming in and out its screen door, the wood smoke thickening. Blacks ate there, but white families knew to order slabs to take home. Eventually we stepped in ourselves, looking for someone we had played football with but didn't visit otherwise. A few adventurers even had a beer before they left.

Before we were quite of age, beer came more easily from Shelby Smith, Reverend Smith's daughter, cigarette-loving, buxom, and hearty, who tended bar at Sarley's. Sarley's was the better restaurant off the square, and we could come to its back door, from the alley, and get a six-pack from her. I think she always let our parents know and refused if they objected; apparently they did not.

The Sunday School I attended—we mostly slipped out after that and left church to the adults, or to those in the choir—was off the northeast corner of the square. We slipped away to a drugstore, ostensibly for a soda, but more to seek a few words with girls, or to stand and thumb magazines, particularly nudist magazines, in black and white on cheap paper, and with small black bars striking out the eyes. Three other churches were within easy reach. The drugstore had reason to open Sunday mornings.

Easter, though, was not just another Sabbath; it was the culmination. That morning, one of the two days in the year when we didn't leave after Sunday School, greenery festooned the altar, with more branches and blossoms swelling around each of the balcony pillars, and amid those blossoms birds sang. Canaries caroled from a dozen or more cages positioned around the sanctuary. Reverend Smith didn't seem to mind but read the Scriptures and delivered his sermon spiritedly, rising above the joyful noise. Shelby led the choir, her hair pulled back to a bun, its red sheen blending with her magenta robe, her voice doing as much as her father's to conduct the service.

There at the focal point of the service, many magnets were pulling—Shelby, Reverend Smith, and Carolie, who also sang in the choir. They were waiting for me; I felt particularly summoned. The whole of the season preceding, beginning imperceptibly after Christmas and building to this moment, led us through weeks of lessons detailing Joseph's selection and adornment, his being sold into Egypt, his exaltation there, his ministry to his brothers during the famine, then Moses, the plagues and the Exodus, the Children of Israel wandering the desert, the very landscape of Lent—with the Old Testament read as a metaphor for the New—then too the sense of Easter as a holiday coming, a change of season, with preparations for dinner whether or not the family went to church, and something new bought for dress and for warmer weather. All this pageantry led to an early Sunrise Service, then to my freighted chance to enter into communion. The Promised Land had been reached; the walls of Jericho were falling, and it was time to open my barricaded heart. But I kept to the balcony rather than venturing the spectacle of immersion in that shallow tub off the altar to the left.

For others it came more naturally, perhaps. But my parents were not religious so had not encouraged me. My grandmother, who thought of herself as Quaker, who subscribed to and sometimes wrote articles for a magazine called *Prevent World War III*, a mushroom cloud on every cover, attended this church— there being no Meeting in town, and Reverend Smith being our neighbor—and she brought me along to Sunday School. But I was already of an age when I was supposed to make up my own mind, and as good as the story sounded, I wasn't convinced. It seemed worse to pretend a faith I didn't have, so I sat in the balcony and watched.

My grandmother lived with us. Two of her sisters lived nearby. We called them the *Tanten*, German for Aunts. One very distinct childhood memory was rising one Sunday morning, walking down the hall to the bathroom, passing my parents' bedroom, and finding them laughing, hugging, and bouncing on their knees on their bed. They were smiling and not a bit disturbed that I saw them. "What happened," I asked. The Sunday paper lay strewn around, its colorful comic pages helter-skelter. They didn't answer right away, but later, downstairs at breakfast, my mother told me Tante Dora, the younger of my grandmother's sisters, had died the night before. She was old and ill, so it wasn't that much a surprise. What it meant of course was that Grandmother could now move in with her remaining sister, the eldest, Tante Magda, and Mother would no longer live under the watchful eye of her mother-in-law.

My cousins' grandmother and her sister lived across the street from where Tante Magda and now Grandmother would live. Carolie's grandmother lived at home with her, and an older couple, the Staubs, with a single daughter older than my parents, lived next door to us. "Go visit the Staubs; they'll be glad to see you," was my mother's frequent urging, as if, and it seems to have been largely true, a few moments' direct contact with a kid growing up on the street was a gift of some importance. With my grandmother and great aunt, Mother's request was more emphatic. I was scheduled to visit them regularly, especially for "German lessons," the two women being from a bilingual immigrant family. For fifteen minutes a day, not every day but through several years, I sat down to bits of German with my grandmother. I memorized paradigms, copied lessons in a notebook, conversed a little, and learned to read that angular German script.

Sometimes Grandmother forgot to put in her false teeth, and her mouth sagged like a hand puppet bowing. Her hearing aid didn't favor the lesson much either. Often she seemed distracted; that's when I'd notice the stacks of magazines and sheet music around her dark room. She had been an instructor of piano in two or three midwestern colleges, had left Chicago that way, first to a college in Kentucky, then one in Missouri. That's where she met my grandfather, a farm boy who played the guitar. He and a couple of brothers made up a Violin, Mandolin, and Guitar Club, and I remember an old photograph of them gathered beneath a college balcony, playing for young women high above. My grandmother, the youngest of five sisters, was the only one who married.

They had all grown up in Chicago, where her other sisters stayed until Tante Magda and Tante Dora joined us. Now Tante Magda would be moving about the living room. She had cracked both hips and her back after turning eighty-five, was blind in one eye and not well sighted in the other. But she remained vigorous, pushing a walker around, doing most of the cooking, and still fondling her painting supplies. I remember a canister of serious brushes. She had studied at the Art Institute and in Europe, had exhibited widely and won a gold medal at the Columbian Exhibition of 1893. Her brushes stood like a full vase of zinnias beside a palette of hardened, darkening oils.

A putto looked down from one corner of her ceiling, a treasure she had brought home from Munich. *"Meine München!"* she'd mutter. In another corner a plaster, seated Dante, a mock-up of a statue for which she had traded paintings of hers. It's in my living room now. And on a bedroom wall, the still life that I've studied hardest. The formal arrangement is all in the lower third. Black grapes that look wet, a cheese knife on a pale table cloth. Two grapes dangle over its blade as if daring to test its edge. When introduced to a famous surrealist film years later, I thought of those grapes and the knife. Beside them a pear, apple, orange, unbroken bun, and decanter of red wine, almost finished. Two empty green glasses. What always got me was light, a smudge of white paint hovering on the back wall of the decanter. All that precision toward the bottom of the canvas, but leaving two thirds as background, dark, looming, impressionistic. Perhaps the back of a chair, just hinted. Perhaps shrubbery, flowering, in beige, gray, and purple, but if so crowding the edge of the table. Born in 1858, Tante Magda was five years younger than Van Gogh, almost a generation younger than Monet and Cézanne, and had studied in Munich not Paris. But something of Impressionism had caught her.

Now bent, short, and shrinking, her hair waist-length but in a bun and retaining hints of yellow, she dominated the house, draped a sheet over the sofa, or davenport as she said, kept her younger sister off center stage, and was far more outspoken and entertaining. "Would you let the Venetian blinds come live in your home?" she inquired while rearranging the curtains behind her sofa. Her answer was, "No, she certainly would not," which disturbed me, her surprising lack of charity, before I caught on. She also kept pressing Reverend Smith to take her dancing.

In a small town with sufficient grandparents, deaths were common, but traffic deaths disfigured my generation. One classmate's car went out of control on the east side of town, killing his sister. Another's went off a curve coming in from the south, killing the younger sister of another friend. We all knew the right front seat was the suicide seat, and, unless driving, we all jockeyed for it. A grade-school sweetheart's younger brother also died in a wreck. At least three more high school classmates died on the highways or back roads soon after graduation. Seat belts were not yet installed, much less required.

Wrecked cars were our memento mori. I remember being urged, one Sunday, to drive north of town to see a freshly wrecked car that had yet to be towed in. We drove out to the crossroad where it sat, next to a wire fencerow, a sprinkling of mulberries, and acres of shimmering, dust-tinged corn, and stared at the twisted metal, the shattered windshield, the motor pushed back toward the driver's lap. At least he had been removed, but small pieces of flesh, mulberry-tinged, clung to the broken glass.

Several years later, Marion discovered a more gaudy death. Marion spent most of his high school years in reform school. When he returned, always briefly, he was an object of wonder, especially in the locker room, where he exhibited tattoos in unusual places. Later, he spent time in the penitentiary and rode with a gang of motorcyclists. He died among them, and the story was that they came to his funeral and sped over his grave, saluting him with pistols. By that time, he had acquired the nickname, Tiny, which he was not.

Perhaps the cyclists' salute was just imagined, a story stolen from the movies. I was long gone by that time. But I've heard of it often enough, confirmed in local lore, and found it reiterated online only a few months ago. The last time I saw Marion, he knelt trimming the sheriff's lawn. The jail, too, was just off the square, and I had paused there one summer afternoon, my windows down, at our single traffic light. Marion's back was to me as he edged a flowerbed. "Hey Marion," I called out, "what'cha doin'?"

"Two years," he said, without even turning around.

Years later, when I searched out the grave of a close friend, one for whom I had been a pallbearer, I found Marion's only a few steps away. Both had small, flat stones. Luther's just held his name and dates. Marion's featured pistons crossed beneath a skull and the legend "Outlaws Forever."

Luther's death galvanized our school. He was popular, a basketball player, doing well in what we called the "solid" courses, and had the flare of an artist. His family had lived along the ravine that edged the African American neighborhood south of Eastwood but moved to a scrap of land several miles south of town.

Approaching sixteen and not getting along with his father, Luther found a job with a commercial sign-maker willing to foster his readiness to work and his artistic talent. Soon Luther had permission to stay in town and sleep at the shop. One October night, he drove himself to a junior varsity football game, borrowing the sign painter's truck. Luther's new patron decided he didn't want to be responsible for that and sent Luther home. A phone call found his father, who came into town. Frustrated and angry, Luther took a cab home instead. By the time his father got home, Luther was dying on the living room floor of a self-inflicted wound from a .22 rifle. At least that was the story, and no investigation ever uncovered another.

The news came to most of us the next morning, to me, during the first period. I'd heard whispers in the hall, and Luther didn't take his seat between Art and me in Geometry. Our teacher retired from the room and came back with the awful announcement. Art, Luther's best friend, went home instantly and stayed in seclusion all that day and the next. Three days later, he played the fiercest football game of his young life. The rest of us drifted through the day in an odd synthesis of grief, exhilaration, and trance. The announcement, never made general, seemed to skip from one class to another and flash into conflagration down the halls. We heard outbursts of sobs from scattered places and found huddles of schoolmates talking in hushed, urgent voices.

Savoring the vicarious thrill of association with tragic life, we monitored our reactions and began to discover how to act. Luther's steady girlfriend stayed in the auditorium all day, crying, with various friends daring to learn around her how one gives comfort to grief. For two days more we made pilgrimages to the funeral home across the street, to see a casket with someone other than a grandparent in it. Luther's body lay at rest, his square features a touch defiant, and with a lump on the side of his head. Many of us went more than once. No one except Art really knew his parents, and they seemed strangers at their son's funeral. It was a funeral for us; we fifteen and sixteen-year-olds were the leading citizens, sweating in our Sunday best that warm October morning, with the casket still open, the long line for viewing, the sobs again from the girls, as each person stood for a moment beside the body. We stood staring death in the face and felt the awe of it.

In the year or so before Luther's death, I had begun to think of Art as my best friend, and after that loss our friendship deepened as I stifled a sense of unearned promotion. Art had a steady girl, as I did not, and was a far better athlete. We shared work, confidences, and took most of the same classes. We forget, later on, how easy it was to talk at one time with a pal of the same sex, intimate talk as boundless as prairie, and as full of currents as our rivers. One late summer afternoon, either the summer before Luther died or the summer after, we were camping with several other friends in woods south of town. It was the last week before football practice, meaning early August. Corn was beginning to turn golden, the landscape browning off, leaves on the scrub oaks crinkling as they lost their green and revealed new color. Somehow the other guys in our party went exploring, but Art and I stayed in camp, preferring the company of each other. We kept a fire smoldering and warmed a couple cans of C rations Art had salvaged from his older brother who had been a paratrooper and then a smoke jumper in western forests. We each had a hatchet, and we sat facing each other astraddle an old rotting log, as fat as horses might have been beneath us, and picked away at it while talking. We spoke of girls, cars, fear of death, football, friends, parents, ideas of God, foreign places, and hunches about college; and we kept it up all afternoon, striking that log almost idly, reducing it to chips, doing the work of Nature over the next several winters and summers, as our talk kept flowing. We found a reservoir that fueled us for years, for a lifetime in fact, whatever the long, serpentine gaps.

Unlike football and track, basketball was a sport for which you could not volunteer. Our coach scouted junior-high gym classes and sidled up to a young man afterward to say, "Son, what size shoes do you wear?" Thus, you were "invited out." Never being selected, I spent four years as manager and statistician. I cleaned and polished two-dozen practice balls daily. I found the hole around a pipe at the top of the storeroom that gave me a cramped view of the girls' locker room. I swept the floor before practices, before games, and during halftime. I packed the trunks with uniforms and saw that they made the bus. Once I packed the keys inside a trunk and the A team had to wear the B team uniforms that were already sweaty. I kept shot charts, writing in the number of every player where he attempted a shot, circling it if good. I passed countless passes to awkward centers improving their hook and jump shots. And in my senior year, I was writing up the games, or games coming, almost daily for the town paper. I never thought to question the value of so serving my classmates and this trim, dark, taciturn, hawk-featured man, who, we heard, had been a champion hurdler in college.

He kept things simple and usually won. He always had a guard who could penetrate and a sturdy forward or two for rebounds. His best player, the guard with the effortless jump shot, was the son of a colleague who taught shop. His team made free throws two-hands, underhanded. It attacked the zone from the baseline after quick passes. He never panicked when behind, never raised his voice or betrayed excitement. His calm in the last minutes probably helped his team pull several games out. Once we were down five points with a timeout and five seconds on the clock and won; but caving in to the tension and hoping to ease defeat by readying things inside, I went ahead into the locker room, only to be surprised some long moments later by the teams' shouts. Then there would be the long bus ride home with a stop at the drive-in. Carolie and the other cheerleaders were already there in their urgent red sweaters, making the place feel as abundant as summer. Coach stood at the bus door, peeling off dollars from a wad in his front pocket. He wore pleated slacks, the first I ever noticed. The money made an impressive bundle, a dollar for each of us, enough for a burger, fries, shake, and small change.

In my last two years I began to scout other teams as well as keep records on our own. At tournaments, Coach kept me with him to watch a second game and to keep a chart on it. Then we drove home in his Olds 88, a car more modern and powerful than that of my parents, skimming the hills and curves in the winter quiet, the cold-looking stars making a shot chart of the heavens on a shot-happy night, the sight of the courthouse dome coming just in time to keep me from nodding off. We must have conversed. "That old peckerwood," he'd say about a player, or maybe a father, but I can't remember what our subjects were, and I remember very little of what he said, except once in a history class when he advised us that smoking was like tossing a quarter out the window, every day.

He was looking out the window, no doubt. He taught that whole class looking out the window, or at the floor. And in my time, he never invited out a black. I never questioned it then but remember Art expressing, quietly, a sense of stifled justice. Eugene, Walter, and several others all played football and ran track. Anyone of them might have been a player. If so, we never found out. Their presence wasn't complete enough in those first years of integration for anyone to pursue the matter.

On trips home years later, I'd run across Coach at a farm sale or county fair. Or I've seen him joining a crowd of older men for morning coffee in a cafe on the square. The one time I made a point of greeting him, our conversation stumbled. Since then I've let him pass, and given the habits of his eyes, I'm not sure he noticed.

High school casts a large shadow over a town and over the memory of its people. Insofar as it conveys us into adulthood, later graduations are anticlimactic. In a town not given to the professions, full-time work comes early; puberty and adulthood crowd closely together. Rumor had one-tenth of my graduating class standing pregnant on the stage. A few girls were already married and another dozen had husbands by the end of that summer. Not quite half of us went on to college and another fair fraction into the service. Almost everyone had a job of some kind, and for many the shift to working full days was barely perceptible. Some simply stopped taking the bus in from the country. Farmers, mechanics, grocers, truck drivers, shop clerks, small-factory workers, local entrepreneurs, inheritors of one small business or another—many classmates found college inessential.

And so was our reunion. Oh, reunions are erratic events. The first one I attended was my twenty-fifth. For it, classmates and a scattering of other friends came from a range of places, including both coasts, but many who'd stayed around town didn't join us. Perhaps their interlocking memories had become too baroque as scenes of youth bled into those of succeeding years, or maybe just too clouded. The afternoon of the reunion, I found my first girlfriend running a Casey's store. Once Francie and I played George and Martha Washington in a grade-school pageant, our selection riveting the class since we were taken to be sweethearts. Much later, as seniors, she had run up in the hall to show me her engagement ring the morning after she got it. And I looked her up when I came back for the reunion, but she didn't come to the dance. Perhaps she and others were shy of bringing their lives to the party, which, if so, is too bad because few were showing off. My brother, who has stayed in town and gone to all his reunions, says the posturing slows radically after the tenth. Still many of us gathered to enjoy drinks, dinner and dance, and a picnic the next day in the park. A group photo placed class officers in the middle once more, even though a mostly new set had displaced them in practice, staying closer to home and so doing the real work of bringing us together.

We entered a charmed circle, sweet enough for its moment. I'd driven six hours to attend and knew one man coming from a town only a half hour from where I started. We met pleasantly and had been teammates but made no move to travel together, nor now to visit once we got back. And, living right off Interstate 80, I invited several classmates known to travel east and west to stop with us, knowing they probably would not.

Still it was a fine event. Two women chastised me for not dancing with them enough; and one, whom I just could not recognize though she challenged me repeatedly, asserting that we had shared classrooms from the second grade on, was probably secretly pleased—she had lost thirty pounds preparing for the party.

Recently a friend saw me at a university bulletin board, studying a notice of an academic conference. "You should offer a paper," she came over to encourage, "it's a good conference." Having gone to the host school, she knew its organizers.

"Well, at least it's close to home," I replied.

"Where's that?" she asked, surprised, and I told her. She said she came from the same town, had gone to my high school—our high school—graduating eight years after I had. But our accidental meeting gave us small means of reunion, for she knew none of my names and I none of hers. Oh, she knew the coach, knew he had learned to "ask out" some blacks, and she knew my two classmates who had returned to teach in our school. But she didn't know of Walter or Eugene, no great surprise. She didn't know of Carolie or Art. She didn't know of Marion or Luther. She didn't know of Carolie's quarterback, who won a scholarship to the state university, or of the guard Carolie married, who starred at West Point. She didn't know of the runner who went into electronics with NASA. Though a musician herself, she didn't know of the pianist who introduced me to "Weekend Monitor," Chris Connor, Bob and Ray, and Ella Fitzgerald, who has won a couple of Grammys by now and has been on "Weekend Monitor" himself. She didn't know of Elaine, who sang with the pianist. She didn't know of our science whiz who went to college on a merit scholarship, was hijacked for a time by Scientology and dropped out. She didn't know any of the still-echoing pantheon that had absorbed me completely only two high-school generations ahead of hers. Barbara's memories must sound as deeply as my own, but they are all but entirely different.

In an Innertube, on the Amazon

One afternoon in early 1962, I stood in the courtyard of the Centro Colombo Americano in Barranquilla, Colombia and met Hunter Thompson. He was unknown to us then, but there he was, a young man, slightly older than I, traveling. I remember chinos and walking shoes, sleeves rolled up, a shirt with red brick in its color, a camera around his neck and another over his shoulder. His suitcase leaned against a cement pillar from which an omnipresent yellow wash was flaking. A separate, smaller case, transparent of purpose, suggested he was a writer. I was a recent English major, and this was not yet an illustration from *Banana Republic*.

Thompson was taller than I, and lean, though less skinny, for I was losing thirty pounds to the heat that year, my first out of college and first in the sub-tropics. Near the Caribbean coast of Colombia, Barranquilla spread around a port dredged from the Magdalena River in the swampy, sandy reaches of the Magdalena delta. Anything as serene as a beach was a dozen miles or more north, the Caribbean as remote to me, practically, as Miami. The season was hot and dry after hot and rainy. Thompson was sweating, having just lugged his bags in from somewhere. Even after months of acclimatization, and with no bags to carry, I too was sticky.

Heat enveloped the unacclimated in a delta of its own with no discernible current. It had touched me first on the tarmac, black and radiant, as I stepped from the plane and, blinking from the glare, sought the nearest shelter. It pursued me to the corner where I waited for the bus, a mirage of shimmering red and yellow; to bed at night with damp sheets twisting around me; to a space behind our school building where boards, a cement mixer, and sand, traces of an expansion project never completed, perhaps never more than begun, leaned against a concrete wall topped with shards of broken glass, and where an iguana blinked his archaic patience.

I'd never known heat like that, and more arresting than the heat itself was its implication of looseness. Always before heat had meant sweltering in Midwestern fields in midsummer, baling hay or hoeing beans and corn. It had meant the first, suffocating, early mornings of high school football practice, in mid-August, when player after player collapsed against the chain link fence after wind sprints, his strength draining from arms and legs through the heaves of an insulted stomach. Getting into shape we called it as our bodies thrown on that old fence made it rattle.

But in Barranquilla the very shapeliness of things was in question. Was that iguana part of the concrete wall or a wayfarer upon it? The air that seemed to cling at midday on the street corner, as if you were wrapped in cellophane and caught under strong lamps, crossed with the scent of oleander and jasmine in the evenings. And the loose-limbed people on the streets, in cotton dresses, baggy pants, short-sleeved shirts, and in a full spectrum of skin colors, from linen to caramel to black, seemed never just walking but sauntering. Neither relief nor penalty for them, heat was their medium.

Against that background, Thompson and I stood alone in the Centro's courtyard, which was basis enough for our meeting. The courtyard was nearly empty—we could hardly ignore each other—and it wasn't long before I'd offered him a couch in the apartment I shared with two other novice teachers, none of us yet a full year out of college.

Thompson had served in the Air Force, mostly with a sports writing assignment for a base newspaper in Florida. And he had spent a year or two in Puerto Rico trying to launch a career in journalism. Now he would jump-start that career as a stringer for several papers as he roamed South America. Barranquilla was near his port of entry. Just that afternoon he had arrived from the Guajira peninsula in northeast Colombia with its Indians and *contrabandistas*.

So Thompson set up his typewriter on a card table in our apartment and spent most of his week with us working on stories. Then he set off up the Magdalena River toward Bogotá; three hundred miles or more with a native crew on a working barge, then at least as much overland, threading through highlands and the Andes, by local bus or donkey, however he could manage. In two months, he wanted to be in Peru, where elections were coming. All this with much less Spanish than I commanded, virtually none at all was my impression.

Though undaunted by the continent, Thompson was not imprudent. He told of arranging for money to be waiting in a series of banks throughout South America and of places to send stories as he wrote them. His dispatches from those times mention an editor and a secretary. A studio in New York developed and stored his photographs, along with the numbered captions he wrote out and filed with them. When he sold a story, as he explained to me with the aplomb of a pro, or a Duke, he could have the appropriate pictures forwarded. Still, setting off as he was doing seemed foolhardy, like tossing an innertube on the Amazon and leaping atop it.

The *contrabandistas* of the Guajira not only provided a point of entry for Thompson's assault on the continent but also on his becoming an author. Their language was their own; Thompson and they hadn't even the hope of Spanish between them. In a dispatch he published later and may have written the week he was with us, he told of the fifty hours he spent among them, drinking contraband Scotch and holding it, more out of wariness than capacity. He wrote of men in loincloths, women in shapeless tunics, the abundance of Scotch, the $300 wristwatches many of them wore, and his truck ride out of the village. "Here was a white man," he says, narrating his arrival by a smuggler's sloop from Aruba:

> with 12 Yankee dollars in his pocket and more than
> $500 of camera gear slung over his shoulders, hauling
> a typewriter, grinning, sweating, no hope of speaking
> the language, no place to stay—and somehow they were
> going to have to deal with me.

My own arrival in Barranquilla seven months earlier was entirely different in tone though rich in shape-shifting incident. The flight from Miami veered west from Barranquilla because a strike of machinists had shut down the airport. Then we found Cartagena, the nearest city to the west, a sixteenth century fortressed, colonial port, "the jewel of the Caribbean," closed too; demonstrating students occupied its runway. Nearing Bogotá, inland, 600 miles farther south, and almost twice as high as Denver, we were told the student strike was over and we would return to Cartagena as soon as we could change planes, which we did, to one that felt refrigerated because minimally pressurized. A young woman sitting near me, whom I recognized later at the university in Barranquilla, smiled apologetically and used an airbag. We landed well after midnight, were hustled through makeshift customs, where I had no occasion to use the sentence I had memorized for the moment—*Yo no llevo nada para vender, pero tengan Uds. mis* Lucky Strikes"; "I have nothing to sell, but take my Lucky Strikes"—and led to a bus for a two hour ride along the coastal road to Barranquilla. Every time we hit a pothole, a few men in front, companions to the driver, sang a mocking ditty ending with the words, *"Alianza para Progreso,"* President Kennedy's idealistic but nonetheless cynical initiative for hemispheric development. The Bay of Pigs debacle was over, and conditions for the Cuban Missile Crisis were building. Latin America held our attention in a way that was, and was felt to be, condescending and dangerous.

I think that bus ride was my first inkling of any such awareness. Our windows were open as we rollicked along that coastal road. It was too dark to make out much of the landscape, just palm trees, shrubbery, jungle-like growth swelling on both sides with occasional breaks on our left, the north side, suggesting the sea. Sea breezes mingled with decay from swamp and jungle. The bus was full of strangers, except for Suzanne, another new teacher, fresh from Vassar, whom I'd met in flight. I can't think of another time and certainly none earlier when I had been so far from home, at such a late hour, hurtling with strangers through the dark, and lacking even the embrace of my language. Strangely, though, I don't remember feeling anxious, but more a sense of expectation, as if I were beginning to breath more ably, and with an idea just dawning that those singers in front of me, "common folks" I probably would have said, "laborers, ill-educated," were truly different individuals, capable of ironic detachment from the political idealism of the Kennedy years with which I identified. Obviously they hadn't been charmed by any whiff of Camelot.

Curiously, too, asthma, a companion from my earliest years, never caught up with me during my two years in the sub-tropics. Not once in Colombia did I need the inhaler I brought along.

One of Thompson's Colombian reports preserves the unforgettable image of a "tall Britisher" standing on a penthouse terrace in Cali, a city in southwestern Colombia, driving golf balls over "the urban peasantry" while doing equal justice to a gin and tonic. That's an image I might have been instructed by that night on the bus, had I been privy to it, not just as warning but as confirmation of all I intended to stand against. I'd gained my draft board's permission to come—the Vietnam build-up had not yet begun; my absence could be afforded—so I went, in my own imagination, with a trace of national assignment. But Thompson's report would prove an omen.

When we arrived in Barranquilla, at around 3 a.m., Suzanne and I shared a taxi to the *Hotel Central*. Not the most obvious place for ignorant gringos, as it turned out, but its name had recommended it. We roused a clerk who could not believe a young man and young woman wandering in off the streets at this late hour really wanted separate rooms, and for the whole night, at least for what remained of it. But we insisted and got them. Each turned out to be more like a barracks. Mine had eight cots, the other seven empty. The wall dividing my room from Suzanne's rose two thirds of the way to a high ceiling, over which, and centered on it exactly, a long bladed fan turned slowly. I fell asleep to the dying down of street noises through wooden shutters and awoke to blazing sun, when I opened those shutters, and to a gringo schoolmaster in a safari shirt, with a taste for gin and tonic, but with rather little Spanish.

Now, most of a school year later, we were still learning to deal with Barranquilla. The wind gave some relief from the heat, though it could turn insistent. In its season it forced sand through the louvered windows of the classrooms in our school, a *colegio*, or elementary and junior high school. The wind's steadiness swayed our world; we were persuaded it made ripples in our toilet. But in the evening the air could turn to balm and you could stroll to the neighborhood "juiceria" as if through bathing fragrance. And the rain in its turn came in early afternoon torrents. Barranquilla's large public market squatted on the riverbank, near sea level, with downtown clumped at its back like a frog on lily pads. Rain water swept off the surrounding low hills, turning the sewerless downtown streets into arroyos, traps for cats, cars, and the unwary. The rain redefined everything for a fresh moment. Then steam rose again as the sun sucked up all that quick wetness.

The residential streets on those low hills were dotted with oleander, jasmine, and bougainvillea. A common scene in the afternoons of the dry season would be a girl, probably the daughter of a maid, with a hose in her hand watering shrubbery and grass worked improbably out of the sand. She seemed as impassive as the iguana, and almost as stable, only her hand flicking the hose from side to side, in no hurry to turn from this task to another.

Someone was always standing on the street, watching. Some men were said to be thieves, keeping an eye on apartments for when residents were absent. Maids routinely slept in single rooms outside houses or apartments; they would be locked out at night and let in again in the morning so that they could not assist, or be forced to assist, *ladrones*. As an unsettled person in a settled neighborhood, I never had enough stuff to be of much interest to a thief; at least no clear attempt was made. Still the Phillips screws around the large casement window on our apartment worked themselves loose every few weeks—someone must have been by at night, loosening them gradually—and I would go around to reset them. The turkey buzzards on roof peaks and telephone poles, just about the only birds around—at least the only ones I remember—signaled the strangeness of the place to me, as did the odd alligator making its way across the playground, or the occasional small herd of cows on our street, drifting from no pasture to no pasture that I could recognize.

Gabriel García Márquez would soon confirm that coastal Colombia lived under the gaze of the *gallinazo,* the turkey buzzard. He offers it frequently as an emblem of the area. In a joke I finally caught the gist of after several tellings, America was likened to the *gallinazo* because of our foreign policy, not just feeding off the *muerte* but tugging entrails from their anuses. Barranquilla was García Márquez's home during much of the fifties. As Macondo changes in *One Hundred Years of Solitude* from a sleepy village to a city swollen on the colonial fortunes of the banana industry, Barranquilla becomes the model for it. He writes himself into the later sections of his book as Gabriel, who with three friends from his early days, clustered around a "wise Catalan" who owned a bookstore there. Those characters become "the first and last friends" of Aureliano, his protagonist. But we did not know any of this then for the novel had yet to be written, nor had we heard of García Márquez, who spent much of that year roaming Faulkner country in Mississippi.

The Alexandria Quartets were the books I carried with me; they provided my way of imagining my new surroundings and its excesses that Thompson was readier to encounter. I could imagine camels hacked apart beside bonfires in the market place, which I approached cautiously, testing my beginner's Spanish. I enjoyed being served *tinto,* rich, thick black coffee laden with sugar, as I opened an account in a local bank or went back to make deposits. I enjoyed having the pesos—at ten to the dollar I was well off, even on a salary of $250 a month, half of which I sent to a bank in the States—and enjoyed sitting in a corner cafe with a local beer, watching the street life saunter around me. I felt there should be a poet of this city too—a Cavafy though I had not heard of him yet and Durrell doesn't name him in the *Quartets*—to justify Barranquilla's steamy back streets by rendering the feel of its cafés and brothels. And of course there would be Justines, still hidden from me but waiting to illuminate the chosen with their rarified seductions and world-weary glamour. The narrator of the first novel of Durrell's *Quartet* happens to be a young British schoolteacher who was learning to deal with Alexandria as I felt I would come to know Barranquilla, by being drawn in to its redolent layers of decadence.

Our school had been founded a generation earlier when many more gringo dependents resided in Barranquilla as in other Latin American cities, and its chief purpose was to educate their children in a familiar manner. Now the student body was about seventy percent Colombian, from its moneyed population, with a sprinkling of children from other Latin American countries and an array of miscellaneous Europeans. I had a Chilean girl in my fourth grade class, a boy from England, another from Holland by way of Brazil. Several families in the school were Swiss German; one was French Canadian, another Bavarian Catholic. And I remember most of my pupils' names—Mauricio, Michael, Raimundo, Simón, Beatríz, Marta, Hernando, Pedro, Gabriel and Alvaro, Magda, Jimmy, Dicky, Leslie, and Maria— not bad after half a century in other classrooms. Those children called me *"Profesor,"* with a rising accent, possibly with a touch of irony. No matter, it became prophecy, perhaps yielding a subtle advantage. For the Colombians, the chief advantage of our school was early mastery of English, making college in the U.S., or shopping in Miami, accessible.

Our pupils had servants. I remember one boy, barely waist high, trying to write out his homework while watching a basketball game in the schoolyard. The wind frustrated him, whipping up the textbook's pages. "Pedro," he called to his chauffeur, a man old enough to be my father, *"cuatro piedras,"* without even looking at Pedro and with no *por favor* added. Poking around, Pedro came up with four stones to hold down the flapping pages. Another day, when I sought to pry information from my class about who had drawn sexually explicit pictures all over the one

North American girl's social studies textbook, I kept them in all recess and was daring to continue their incarceration through a two-hour lunch period and siesta, when a string of maids arrived at the schoolroom door bearing hot meals. Soon I was the only one hungry, and I remember one boy, dissatisfied with the tray provided by his grandmotherly maid, ordering her to the corner *tienda*: "Bring me a sandwich and a coke," he ordered. And she did.

Perhaps Thompson would have found a better solution. He might have initiated a contest to see who could get their drawings right and in the ensuing enthusiasm trick the defacer into betraying himself. Suffice it to say a solution as cunning as that was as distant from me as Durrell's Alexandria. My pupils and their parents hardly had to deal with me; I would serve their purposes and be gone soon enough. But I was working strange currents and learning by improvising.

I might have come with the Peace Corps. That would have been less likely for Thompson. A journalist of his sort would hardly develop from an idealistic joiner. The Peace Corps was just getting under way at that time, and one of the first groups in the field came to Colombia a few months after I did. Often people discovering I was in Colombia then assume I was a member. But I wasn't that kind of joiner either. With no grand purpose in mind, I thought teaching abroad would be a fine way of following through on my English major, which seemed a sufficient emblem of virtue and awareness. Had not J. D. Salinger characterized Frannie positively just by calling her "an English major"? If irony underscored his usage, I failed to notice. Instead, I found addresses for American Schools in Paris, Geneva, and Rome, and wrote them. And I wrote Barranquilla because of a flyer that had come to my college. Barranquilla answered. In that slow week between final exams and graduation, after

I'd almost forgotten my inquiry, I received a telegram: "If still interested, wire back"—and I did. An earlier recruit must have got a better offer. Then, after writing a letter on my "philosophy of education," which I had to improvise since I had next to nothing to base one upon, I found myself employed.

Today what most dominates our image of Colombia, aside from García Márquez, is violence and drug traffic. In 1962 in a petty way, contraband was everywhere: wristwatches, cigarettes, and Scotch, not bourbon for some reason, but Scotch, and gin. A man would work our neighborhood like a paper route and make regular deliveries if we wished. I knew of marijuana and worse, but I didn't think much about it and knew few who did. Beer and gin had been our drugs of choice through college. Soon we would all learn about "Colombian Gold," but though the system for its exportation must have been developing, I was in the dark about it. I may have been an English major, but I wasn't "beat." Nor did Thompson give any sign of being on drugs, alert to them, or investigating drug traffic.

What we all knew a little about was *la Violencia*. Nearly all reports agree that the assassination in 1948 of Jorge Gaitán, a popular liberal politician, was catalyst for renewing Colombia's prolonged political violence. Gaitán had been mayor of Bogotá and a possible candidate for the presidency. The revenge of the masses that day, costing hundreds of lives, is remembered as the *Bogotazo*. But murder and ambush have long plagued Colombia. Between 1946 and 1966, *la Violencia* took an estimated quarter million lives. That's about five times the number recorded on the Vietnam War Memorial and from a country with roughly one tenth our population. Furthermore, that loss came within memory of a turn-of-the-century civil war that cost another hundred thousand lives and of a bloody labor conflict in the late twenties that had centered on the banana-growing region just east of Barranquilla. Gaitán's report to Congress on that violence and his pin-pointing blame on the government's support of United Fruit interests had launched his presidential aspirations. There has been good reason for the *gallinazo* to live well in Colombia.

In the fifties, during the height of *la Violencia,* Colombians endured two dictatorships, one elected, the other military. In 1950, the Liberal Party, divided and intimidated after Gaitán's murder, could field no presidential candidate and Laureano Gomez, a Conservative extremist with Falangist convictions, took office. He began to purge the country of Liberal office holders, turning the police and army against large portions of the population. This tactic stimulated guerilla activity and the country again came close to civil war. In 1953, a general, Rojas Pinilla, seized power and promised to quell the violence. To some extent he managed, but his dictatorship inspired more, and after several savage blunders that provoked the opposition of even the Catholic Church, he was forced from office. Then the oligarchs of the Liberal and Conservative parties agreed on a National Front in which offices down to the local level would be distributed equally, with the presidency alternating from one party to the other every four years, ending in the hands of the Conservatives.

In 1962, we were awaiting the first national election under this new system. Everyone was apprehensive. People I met were just beginning to feel they could speak openly of politics; even at home they had feared an informer lurking by an open window. The principle of equal distribution of office, coupled with a Colombian tradition of family identification with party extending through generations, made politics more a matter of nomination than of election. You were born to your party and chose your candidate within it, as García Márquez's novels all take for granted. Less certain was your relatively liberal or conservative stance within your party. Pinilla was already back in the land, his status as citizen disputed, but testing things anyway with a rump candidacy of his own. As Thompson observed, he was probably the only deposed dictator living openly again in the capital city from which he had been so recently driven, and with his phone number listed.

By the early sixties, the violence Pinilla had both attacked and perpetuated was mostly acted out in rural areas with small groups under several banners gaining momentary advantage over each other, and with outright banditry as much a motive as any political agenda. FARC and similar revolutionary groups were in their infancy. But occasionally a bus would be stopped on a country road and everyone on it gunned down, or a dozen men from a particular village would each lose an ear. Many of the barmaids and shoeshine boys in Barranquilla said they had come to the coast as refugees from *la Violencia,* for the worst of it had always been played out in the interior. This was an interior into which Thompson was heading and through which Peace Corps workers were already scattered. Meanwhile I was teaching children of the well off on the northern coast of Colombia.

As the *profesor,* I watched the apprentice writer work. Our cook's boyfriend distributed a local beer and supplied us with cases of it. With Thompson that week, we went through one or two extra. While we were teaching, he wrote, unfazed by our modest quarters, our wobbly card table, straight-backed chair, the heat, the lack of air conditioning, and our couch that was no featherbed. Pages piled up on the card table; others filled the wastebasket. He hit his keys sharply: on the white water of the open page, he paddled decisively.

During intermissions, we talked about college, the Army and Air Force, and writers and writing. We'd come home from school, shuck our ties, open our short-sleeved white shirts, and a beer, and talk. Henry Miller was Thompson's favorite writer.

He spoke of Miller as a neighbor in Big Sur, which was only a name to me. He thought of writers as actors shaping events of consequence around them. He was insistent on getting into the world, being part of the game, not just observing but enlivening its strange corners. Not only those Indians in the remote Guajira, but the world at large would have to deal with him, and with his skewing, by his active presence, the previously accepted format. He embodied something of an existentialist ethic which, by emanating more from Yankee initiative than from despair of cosmic purpose and justice, ran more than a little toward caricature. But he was committed, and writing.

I in turn told tales of our school such as how a teacher the semester before, who had lasted only that term, had slain an iguana for his third grade class. Cort had insisted on turtleneck sweaters, black wool as I remember them, which must have been hell in the heat. Image obviously mattered. Perhaps he thought of himself as beat. He spoke often of his motorcycle. And one day, on the playground at recess, he saw that iguana resting on the concrete wall. To him, it was a menace and he assured his charges, third graders, he would deliver them from it. Rummaging around in the scrap lumber from the abandoned construction project, he found a piece of two-by-four and hefted it, cracking it experimentally across his open palm. Then he advanced on the poor beast in a sideways two-step, as if fencing or practicing karate. His weapon flailed in the air. The iguana barely turned its head. It was about the size of a squirrel and six hundred times slower. "Whap, whap," Cort smashed him, and a reptile tumbled off the wall to rot in the weeds beside it. Cort's boys, as unthreatened by an iguana as I might have been by a bunny, didn't say a word; they just turned their backs and shuffled off to the basketball court. And why hadn't I intervened, I wondered to myself, without confessing my self-doubt to Thompson.

Thompson carried an album with him, something oddly extra to lug around a continent and betraying his own unexpected vulnerability. I remember a black, loose-leaf binder with clippings from post newspapers and other mementos, among them several glossy color photographs of his home in Big Sur and of landscape and people there, including Miller. No parents or siblings that I can remember, but the homestead he had been making, he said, with lush shots of the meadows and mountains around it, and of his girlfriend. In one stunning photograph, she runs naked through a meadow, stride for stride with a palomino, her breasts high, her stride strong and even, two beautiful blond manes flowing. I picked up Thompson's binder several times that week to check her out again.

Meanwhile, I was negotiating vulnerabilities of my own, among them, how to stand up day after day as a reasonable teacher. Part of the oddity of our school had to do with the idealism of our director who, having arrived only the year before, had stumbled onto a staff that did not altogether charm him, and who, to fill vacancies, advertised at a couple of dozen liberal arts colleges rather than through the clearing agency in Washington, which would have insisted on certification and teaching experience. Partially we were there as malleable youngsters who could share daydreams and drinking time with him. Partially we were to bring a touch of Andover to Barranquilla, with its sandy flats, its glass shards embedded atop so many concrete walls, its iguanas lost in odd corners of the schoolyard, and *gallinazos* soaring above us, especially, I noticed, over small children playing basketball on the playground.

Our director wanted ours to be a cosmopolitan school with several languages embedded in our teaching. He got German added to the elective curriculum that year, and he organized a Spanish class for his gringo teachers. To that end he arranged for Professor Cuello to sit with us for an afternoon or two

50

each week and introduce his fresh-out-of-college gringo staff to the treasures of Spanish poetry. Not a one of us had been a Spanish major.

Professor Cuello made the rounds of several schools to secure a small living. He had been a student at Salamanca and now taught religion to the children in our school. A couple of days each week, he drilled groups of our pupils then bussed off to another school on his rounds, teaching Colombian history or Spanish grammar elsewhere. Rarely in a hurry, he seemed pleased to sit with us and crack the window on a vanishing world that he loved.

It was as if, were our roles reversed, I were to begin with Wyatt and Surrey and push on to Donne and Herbert. I remember trudging through some *Coplas* of Jorge Manrique but failing to rise to their moral concerns. I remember better a lesson the flirtatious Colombian third grade teacher whispered to me, a ditty the burden of which was that I should "plant a tree, raise a son, and write a book"—*plantar un arbol, criar un hijo, escribir un libro.* Her point in part was that I should learn to roll the Spanish "rrrs" and make them my own, *escrribirrr un librro.* "What about a daughter?" I did have the wit to ask, but that got us nowhere, perhaps because I missed her hints of what I should roll and where my tree might be planted.

How could it be that I fixed instead on Professor Cuello's fine story of Frey Luis de Leon's being hauled away by the Inquisition, imprisoned for five years, then returning to his classroom in Salamanca where students on wooden benches heard him intone, "As we were saying yesterday" as he strode to the front of the hall? His words rang out in Latin, *hesterna dia.* I sought those benches out a couple of decades later when I made it to Salamanca and found them so narrow and rough-hewn that they were sure to hold a class's attention by their discomfort. But what really caught my attention, inexplicably, those Barranquilla afternoons was the *Serranilla de la Finojosa* by the Marqúes de Santillana. Why? Only the mysteries of poetry can answer that.

> *Moza tan fermosa*
> *non vi en la frontera*
> *como una vaquera*
> *de la Finojosa. . . .*

A couple of those "f's" have changed to "h," making it *hermosa* and *Hinojosa,* as I found once on a map. The *serranilla,* related to the *pastourelle* of medieval French convention, encourages a knight to dally with a pretty country girl, as I might have with our third grade teacher, had I been a knight and she not a woman who would have minced me. The poem, in fact, is also a warning for it is not so innocent as to be without irony, especially when the woman gets the better of the knight. But the poem sounds innocent with its tripping meter and two-syllable rhymes. A touch of Dr. Seuss dampens its dignity. *Frontera, vaquera; moza, fermosa,* and *Finojosa* are typical of the run of it. Nevertheless it stuck with me, and years later I realized that with hardly any effort, except to have read it over many times, I had all six stanzas memorized. For one late evening, pushing the boundaries of welcome at a good party, I found myself reciting this poem with Dr. Ignacio Ponseti, a man a generation older than I and from Barcelona, a doctor who had crossed the Pyrennes with Antonio Machado and remnants of the Republican army in 1936 and renewed his career years later in Iowa City where he became famous for his patient, non-surgical correction of clubfeet in children. The song-like poem had colonized a corner of my mind, and his too, for it breathes a serenity that no amount of the far-fetched can compromise.

> *Faciendo la via*
> *del Calatraveño*
> *a Santa Maria,*
> *vencido del sueño*

por tierra fragosa
perdí la carrera
do vi la vaquera
de la Finojosa.

Passing from one place to another over variations in fragrant landscape as slight but noticeable as moving back and forth from *abab* to *abba* quatrains, and conquered by sleep, a knight loses his way and sees the cowgirl of *Finojosa*. On a green plain of "roses and flowers," she guards livestock with other cowgirls whom she outshines since no spring flowers could match her beauty. The subjunctive turns, as the two approach each other, are ravishing for their deflection of the obvious—that each one recognizes, precisely, the nature and role of the other. When they finally speak, he asks, slyly, "Where is the cowgirl of *Finojosa?*" as if she did not stand before him. And she, in parallel third person, as knowingly replies, "She knows well your desire but is in no need of love, nor does she expect any." And that, with its implied "so there!" ends the poem, and the flirtation. I cannot count the number of times that poem has risen to mind, "for no rhyme nor reason" as my father liked to say.

I'd entered a schoolroom lacking textbooks for math or English. But the kids had mastered addition and subtraction the year before, so we took up multiplication, division, and fractions. As for English grammar, we had blackboards and, recalling some elementary and junior high instruction, I thought we could diagram sentences.

I structured most of that first year as competition, which is curious to remember. I divided the class into two teams and sent representatives to the board in relay, either to write out a times table or diagram a sentence. "The sevens," I'd shout, and two competitors would race from their seats to write out the whole table on the board, tables we extended gradually to "12 x 12," then "13 x 13."

I seldom had to worry about alertness. Those kids were noisy champions and critics of each other. But why that stratagem in the first place? Was it the only means I could think of to hold their attention and to keep, without textbooks, at the lessons expected? I remember no lack of will to divide the room and start the game afresh. Enough of my students were so eager to play that often when I wanted to pause, to turn their attention to a new piece of instruction, or simply to close one lesson and open another, I resorted to whacking a yardstick across the top of my desk, its limber, whipping action making a prolonged "crack," which worked well until my small violence lost its surprise and the kids egged me on to repeat it. But I also remember, reluctantly, that some children were less eager than others and surely would have welcomed less aggressive methods had I been able to imagine them. They floundered while I floated with the combatants. In fact, I cannot remember now the number of pupils I had, and no old grade book remains to help me. I suspect that those names I recited earlier are mostly of the willing, with the others—and how many more were they? three or four? twice that many? my poor iguanas—struck from my memory and so to a degree of oblivion.

Sentence diagramming was a more deliberative contest. It allowed for nuances of interpretation and prompted more flourish. I found I remembered less than I thought, and we quickly ran into complexities that I could not resolve. But I had a knack for tolerating doubt, even entertaining it, and allowing solutions to evolve from our communal scrutiny of sentences. So gradually I tutored all sorts of fourth graders, with Spanish their mother tongue, or *costeño* as they said, with pride, of their coastal deviations from Bogotá—*un fóforo* [match], *do fóforo* rather than *un fósforo, dos fósforos* being their ritual example—to diagram sentences they would never utter in English, or in any other language:

> When you cross the Mississippi for the first time, with Mauricio and Beatriz and Maria, all of you singing, "Oh Carmina, don't you cry for me," and with Maria, on your right, keeping time with a spoon on the dashboard of your car, don't forget to remember, in one corner of your mind, your grandmother, who had a little something to do with making all this possible, however far that may have been from her intentions.

I was observing too, while my charges worked at the board, that the apparent rainbow spirit of their population had its limits, that Maria the Chilean, Mauricio's closest challenger, could always be squelched by his reminder that she was *mas negra* than he, though the taunt was even more likely to come from blonde Beatríz, and you could hear the same words on the streets of any neighborhood. Like the sun, such watchfulness was ever present.

When I wasn't drilling the fourth graders, in everything they took but Spanish, I found myself flattered into teaching a university class in the *Escuela Superior de Idiomas,* a division of the *Universidad de Atlántico.* Professor Asa, its director, hired Barry, my Harvard roommate first; then he added me. Most of the students were older than we, and several were hoping for Fulbrights and other awards to the U.S., though the real mission of the school was to train bilingual office workers. Its student body featured many of the *mas negro,* for whom I was asked to teach a preparatory course in American literature and culture.

My English major training was less to the point than one might imagine. Henry Miller was no hero of mine, nor Kerouac. But neither of those writers would have been feasible, not even Steinbeck, for the students didn't have the texts. The school had hardly any library, and close reading, the only skill I had acquired in college, would have to be performed on whatever I could type out and mimeograph.

I thought to begin with *Prufrock*. Images of him entertained by Durrell's Justine captivated me without my worrying about whether Eliot would ever have risked Alexandria, or have even heard of Barranquilla. Nor did I consider, seriously, what those students were likely to think of Prufrock. Blind to those contingencies, I was eloquent and excited and soaring on wings of self-assignment. I knew, or thought I knew the pathos of Eliot's drawing rooms with their tepid tea and ices rather than our markets and bars, our local beer, contraband Scotch, and *aguardiente* with salt and lemon; and I thought it important to tell them all I imagined.

Alas, I soared alone. It took a couple of weeks to learn how silly my flight, while my Spanish stirred and I found friends from class who spent afternoons and evenings with me, over coffee and beer, amid struggling conversations, more in English than Spanish for they were well ahead of me; but they weren't even beginning to follow my lectures. And others, like the young woman on the Avianca flight, who felt it improper to come forward with a question or complaint, were even more completely left out, or just found the whole performance irrelevant.

Some of those evenings Ignacio would take me out with his friends, also from the university but now graduates. Americo was bell captain at the tourist hotel near our school. Luis seemed to have spent a little time in Cuba and was looking forward to a year in Russia; or maybe it was the other way around. We'd huddle around a table in a cafe, drink beer and talk politics. That's where I heard the joke about American foreign policy in the image of the *gallinazo*. And I heard about a Colombian priest who was a guerilla in the Colombian interior and would soon be killed there. It would be more precise to say I heard a great deal but understood only some of it. One evening a barmaid came up to me in a quiet moment and asked whether I desired her attentions. *"Quieres fookie-fookie?"* she asked. I shrugged and said sorry, *"No comprendo."* She repeated herself and I did too. The third time, exasperated, waving her arms, she blurted out *"Fookie-fookie, es una palabra internacional!"*

But I adjusted. I suggested my university students buy the foreign edition of *Time* magazine so we could read about current events in a contemporary idiom and talk politics. The two or three peso cost, however, proved prohibitive for them. Some of those same students rioted and burned buses later that term when the fare went up the equivalent of a U.S. nickel. Soon I was writing dialogues in English for everyday situations and running those off on mimeograph, spending hour upon hour in preparation, and learning some Spanish.

One weekend Ignacio took me to Ciénaga, to visit an uncle. About a million people lived in the coastal cities of Cartagena, Barranquilla, Ciénaga, and Santa Marta, all strung within 200 kilometers, west to east, along the Caribbean coast. Ciénaga is the smallest of them and the banana capital of Colombia. It is the focus of García Márquez's story as the United Fruit empire swells, leading to the banana workers' strike of 1928 and the resulting violence that ended with a long train load of corpses hauled from Macondo. His narrative is based on an actual confrontation between the Colombian Army and striking workers at the train station in Ciénaga. In an appallingly manipulated and one-sided conflict between disadvantaged soldiers and even more disadvantaged workers, with the army summoned to enforce the United Fruit interests of its banana republic, the army had opened fire. One account is entitled *La Masacre en las Bananeras*. The number of victims varies from nine to over three thousand. Be moderate and imagine hundreds. Gaitán's emergence as a national political figure is largely identified with his investigation of the massacre and his report to the Colombian Senate the following year. And García Márquez was accepted as a voice for his people in large part too for having found the truth of legend in that story.

Ciénaga, which means swamp or marsh, is a resonant and tragic name in Colombia. To me it seemed a sleepy town much smaller than its atlas listing of over 20,000. There were clusters of houses and shops, streets powdered with dust into which our shoes sank, and no town center by which I might orient myself. Nor were there sidewalks; houses defined the street edges. A small thatch lean-to stood on the beach under coconut trees, but no one was enjoying it.

Ignacio's uncle lived in a small house, several streets in from the beach, on a corner I saw no way of telling from any other. We had dinner with a family that included a pretty cousin close to our age and her equally pretty girlfriend from across the street. Soon we were improvising a party. We placed a phonograph in an open, screenless window, the speakers street side, and danced in the dust while Ignacio's uncle served Scotch without stopping. Everyone urged me to eat more, drink more, and to dance and dance. They insisted on my having a good time and developed a sudden affection for my middle name, which proved almost a pun on their imperative: "Dance, Bailey, dance,"—"Baile! Bailey, baile!"

In a way, Ignacio and I had come courting, though that hadn't dawned on me, and perhaps not even on him. Whether he, the tall, dark, gallant cousin from the larger city was more the focus of interest, or whether I was, as the polite, restrained, but slightly exotic North American, I cannot be sure. The summer warmth of the evening buoyed us. Caribbean breezes freshened the dusty street. The girls prompted us generously, dancing with themselves, until Ignacio fell in with them and drew me along. It was a mixture of early rock and roll, the twist, and the *cumbia*, a stirring, sensual, serpentine dance with African roots, featuring bandanas and candles, at which I was hopeless though I found it utterly loosening. I cannot remember refusing a single drink, or dance either, after a while. Every so often the girls retreated inside to return in fresh dresses. I have the impression that we saw their entire wardrobe that night, with implications that still make me blush, and that their smiles were cousin to stars twinkling over the Caribbean. But gradually our energy ebbed. Dancing drew closer, interspersed with quieter conversation. Then the girls withdrew for the night and Ignacio and I found places to sleep, me on a couch in the living room, him on a picnic table outside the back door. For decades thereafter I was ineligible as a blood donor for having spent a night under thatch by the Caribbean. Sleep was easy to find, though, and I woke in the morning to the persistent buzz of flies. All that fried food of the evening before, strips of meat, vegetables with rice, *plátano*, and the body heat, and liquor. We had partied close to a massacre site of which I knew nothing though my country was implicated. I had to wait to read García Márquez.

A more serious flirtation with violence had occurred on an earlier weekend when Suzanne, Barry, and I took a bus past Ciénaga to Santa Marta then taxied up into the mountains just south of there. The founder of our school had a home in the mountains above Santa Marta which he had made available to us, and we heard that if we hiked up the mountain, we'd come to an army outpost at the top and from there could see snow peaks to the south, Colombia's Sierra Nevadas. Our second morning, we set out walking, on a twisting road, ever upward, through the humid and imposing rain forest, with immense trees wreathed in vines blocking out the sky overhead. By noon, we knew we were in for a long walk and could see no evidence of the way clearing before us. Suddenly an open-bedded truck full of men on holiday came along. They offered us a ride, which we accepted, and within half an hour we were at the post, feeling a welcome chill and staring at snow peaks in the distance.

On the way down, when the truck dropped us off, the driver demanded three hundred pesos, which the three of us could pool together but without much left. We were caught off guard and protested, then haggled. The driver would settle for one of our cameras, or a watch. We finally gave him a hundred pesos and walked away, abandoning the argument. Several hours later, we heard the truck return, then belligerent voices, and our driver at the door. He had been refreshed by a few beers and by relating his grievance to friends, and he carried a rifle. Suzanne confronted him first. Her Spanish was best; at least that was our excuse, and perhaps it proved a sobering tactic for the outraged to encounter a young woman. Gradually things were said that needed to be said; anger quieted. The driver's friends intervened; it became clear we weren't rich but merely miscalculating gringos. At that point, we rallied with another hundred pesos and escaped anything more serious.

To me, the saddest passage in Thompson's several articles from the period comes from the same piece that mentions the "Britisher" driving his golf balls over "the urban peasantry." A page later he was quoting me:

> A traveler in South America gets one shock after another at the stance generally taken by his fellow gringos—and sometimes a worse shock at the stance he takes himself. One young American put it this way: "I came down here a real gung-ho liberal, I wanted to get close to these people and help them—but in six months I turned into a hardnosed conservative. These people don't know what I'm talking about, they won't help themselves, and all they want is my money."

He must have taken good notes, or had a fine memory. "Gung-ho" and "hardnosed" would have been part of my vocabulary, brought glibly from college, like "tough-minded," that last a virtue we had supposedly earned, even though ignorant of the loosening elasticity of Latin America that eddied and danced around us while we lost our insistence. In any case, Thompson preserved a frustration I remember. I was not yet twenty-three. The first presumption is that I was there to help at all, that we North Americans knew what they needed and what we should be talking about: how to diagram an English sentence, for example, or the travails of Prufrock. But that was the assumption of the Kennedy era, and of the Peace Corps, and remains our inheritance. It was implicit in Thompson's stance as well. Would those Indians of the Guajira, or any other Latin Americans really have had to deal with him had he not so obviously been a representative, not of the weightier—Vallejo, Mistral, Neruda, Borges, and others were laying that assumption to rest—but merely of the upscale and more militarily powerful culture?

Later that year we would be anxiously watching the Cuban Missile Crisis. As the crisis grew, I felt stranded; and one of my more striking though selfish worries was what would happen to us if bombs laid waste North America and we, suddenly, represented nothing? Of course the Colombians had a way of placing me and what I was "talking about," and if what they wanted most was my money, that is what I most concretely had to offer. My best offering otherwise was probably the sustained example, sometimes the spectacle, of a young man with some sense and more energy beginning to float with, more than thrash upon, the classroom's roiling water.

Back in Barranquilla, Ignacio liked shepherding us to various downtown bars. He knew his way around and we paid for the beer. Thompson insisted on going one night and wanted pictures. We took a table in a small courtyard, alongside a dance floor, at the *Place Pigalle,* stolen, I suppose, from someone's memory of Paris, or perhaps at the "Little Bird," the *Pajarito.* Suddenly Thompson got out his camera, climbed on the table and started shooting. I feared a riot, for those bars doubled as brothels. The groups of men around us were not negligible. Occasionally I'd recognize a school father among them. Our director, who liked these evenings as much as any of us and who also urged siesta-long lunches with gin and tonics at the tourist hotel before returning to afternoon classes, was uneasy. But Ignacio seemed amused. "Hey, Gringo, you want a picture," he was laughing. Thompson took several. The next morning, Barry, whose Spanish was better than mine, escorted Thompson to the docks and negotiated his passage into the interior. And I've never seen him since, except once, more than twenty years later, from the back row of the ballroom of Iowa's Memorial Union where he kept us waiting well over an hour for his lecture-performance.

I was remembering Colombia of course, and remembering, the evening jasmine overpowers the midday sun; the pleasures of dancing in Ciénaga displace the expressions on the faces of the girls with their possible expectations, or those of some men of Ciénaga who tried to enlighten me about the United Fruit Company and the massacre my government had sponsored. My sense of adventure as a beginning teacher outweighs moments when I was more like the tall Englishman driving golf balls off his balcony. Or I think of afternoons roaming around downtown, enjoying *tinto* and *cerveza* with friends from the university, in one of those small courtyards with moss in a corner and a trickle of fountain, where the beer was cold and the talk among young men with dreams intimate. When I leave, I stop at my favorite bookstore, a small one with international newspapers and books from English and German publishers as well as from Latin America. Overhead on a neglected shelf, I discover the folio, faux leather-bound, eighteenth edition of the *Diccionario de la Lengua Española,* 1956, from Spain's *Real Academia.* It was their most recent, and I spring for it, which takes beer money for the next several weeks, for I admired all those words I would never possess but toward which I did and do feel friendly. I still have it, and whether true or not, I think of that shop as that of the "wise Catalan."

Much else of course had happened. I had spent those twenty-plus years as a professor. To many students, and to quite a few colleagues, Thompson had been a guide through the sixties and seventies. One student I knew had written a master's thesis about him and had been stood up twice for interviews. I enjoyed telling him how years after my time in Colombia, after going to a movie in Los Angeles, I had entered a tavern and found that photo of the palomino and the running, naked woman blown up as a life-size mural on the wall behind the bar. "Your guess is as good as mine," I remember saying to my younger friend, "but the place wasn't called 'Hunter's.'"

Someone Is Leaving:
A Ghost Story

My first night in Gabon, while Jenny lay in bed recovering from flu, several of her friends took me out to visit their discos, then to continue, after midnight, to a *bwiti*. A *bwiti* is a privately arranged masked dance to honor the dead and to end a period of mourning. It would be held around a small, ceremonial lodge with a low, thatched roof, an open front, and deep, dark interior. Standing in front of one, even at midday, I was unable to discern shapes at the far end. And to get there, we would walk away from the last disco, through the *quartier* on the far edge of town, along a path that seemed determined to lead us into the forest. I had already seen one such small hole in the forest wall and had been told it started the footpath to Sindara, then to Lambarene, the home of Dr. Schweitzer's hospital, over two hundred kilometers north and west, back toward the coast, and more than halfway back to the equator. But we never got to the *bwiti* because the last disco seemed too compelling for my hosts. Its strobe lights lifted us to motion as did the music and the beer. Dorothee, a 21-year-old single mother in the extended family that had "adopted" Jenny, asked me to dance. That is, Alato came over and said, "Dorothee wants to dance with Jenny's father." She moved well in the only language we could share. The strobe lights made her white shirt glow against her dark skin, drawing out overtones of purple.

Around one o'clock my hosts headed home, and the *bwiti* had not been mentioned for hours. As we emerged from the disco, we felt the chill of night air on our skin. We stood on the road and toyed with possibilities. Looking up, I hoped to locate the Southern Cross, this being my first time below the equator, but all was shadows. The men stood, hands in pockets, voices low, Alato drawing lines with his shoe in the dust. There were a few exchanges among my companions, and with some younger men hanging around the door of the disco. It seemed clear that no one really wanted to continue into the dark.

My hosts suggested I go on with Monica, a Peace Corps companion of Jenny's, and pointed out the path we could follow "until we came to the drums." I would be welcome since I was a visitor, as they, apparently, felt they were not. It was the end of a long day and they had every reason to be tired. They had been away from their wives all evening. Monica would be welcome for the same reason as I, "even though she is a woman," which introduced another uncertainty. Monica and I started into the forest. With every step we felt the darkness cover more of our retreat. We heard owls, or something like owls, but no drums, and after a few turns on the path, we too headed home.

Monica and Jenny lived half a mile apart along a dirt road that followed a river. Monica insisted on showing me the way. I resisted her invitation, and she resisted my resistance. The villagers would expect it. She couldn't leave me, a stranger to the village, and a guest, alone on the road; that would be noticed. Besides, no one walks home alone after a *bwiti*. "What about you?" I asked. She would be okay. She knew the roads; she no longer carried a flashlight, and ghosts had no reason to concern themselves with a foreign girl trying to be helpful in their country. She felt at ease with the young men around the disco and expected no trouble from them. Surprised to find her reasons convincing, I got escorted home by a young woman for the first time in my life.

An hour or so later, I awoke to a face staring down at me. It was a young black woman's face, with high cheekbones, short black hair, and dark eyes. She wore a white turban with blue dots. My mosquito netting seemed to have dissolved to reveal her quiet, observant presence. "Jenny," I called. The figure receded from me, gliding on the apparently weightless bulk of a robed body, but without legs, or at least without feet so far as I could tell. I rose to follow and turned on the light in the main room, which was empty. Both the front and back doors were closed but unlocked, though Jenny was in the habit of locking both at night and I had only entered by one of them. I turned on all the lights and woke her. Jenny checked the doors then returned to bed, appallingly soon I thought. I played solitaire for a while, then lighted a candle, took it into my room, and sat watching it flicker before blowing it out and pulling the netting around me. Before I could blow the candle out, I had to convince myself that I feared setting the netting on fire.

Gabon straddles the equator on the west coast of Africa. In June, 1992, I flew there to visit my daughter, Jenny, who was completing her second year with the Peace Corps. Its coastal capital, Libreville, lies about a degree off the equator to the north; Mimongo, the inland village to which Jenny was assigned, is about two degrees to the south. A longitudinal line arcing north from Mimongo could add Tripoli, Rome, Venice, Prague, and Berlin to its string and not waver much from exact. A line of latitude could reach Belem at the mouth of the Amazon, skirt Papua, New Guinea, to the north, bisect Indonesia, and enter Africa through Nairobi before returning to Mimongo, nearly 3000 feet above sea level in the forested highlands of Gabon.

My way in to Mimongo had been by air, then by truck. A jet from Libreville touched down on packed red dirt outside Mouila, the provincial capital nearest Mimongo, and rolled to a stop well away from the terminal, all poured concrete, unfinished, merely a shell. Recently the government had had money for Mouila, enough to begin the terminal. Then the money stopped. Now boys chased each other through its dusty vaults, kicking a makeshift ball, skidding and doing wheelies on their bikes. In one corner a large scale stood ready for weighing baggage. In another, a check-in counter, unattended except just before flights, bore the deep stains of grease from the fast food lunches of Gabon, fatty, barbecued beef carried away in newspaper. Flies cruised like miniature *gallinazos*. A tank stood close to the terminal, with military trucks around and about. A military plane waited on the field. Uniformed soldiers made themselves evident, a few well armed. A cluster of civilians and soldiers gathered by the steps of the plane as I descended.

I caught sight of Jenny first from my window as we taxied in. She has high cheekbones, short black hair, deep dark eyes, and some rose in her complexion. Her aunt had called her the child with grown-up hands, noting her slender fingers, dexterous from babyhood on. I dwelt more on her eyes, pensive, deep as espresso, and, I always thought, ageless. She wore jeans and a red, short-sleeved shirt. "You look wonderful," I said, as I caught sight of her at the foot of the stairs and opened my arms. It would have been more accurate to say she looked fashionably gaunt. The flu was catching up with her although the first signs were equally of malaria, floating as always within her system, held in check by a weekly tablet of Fanzidar. It was the end of her school year and the end of her two-year assignment. Within two weeks, she would be leaving her village, leaving the home and sense of family she had made for herself there; and I had just flown in to complicate her last days in Mimongo.

Soon we were leaving Mouila and rising into the highlands north of the river, the Ngounie. Jenny and I occupied the front seat of a Toyota pickup with its driver. On the way out of town, he stopped at a bakery and bought a long, French-style baguette. He laid it half wrapped on the dashboard in front of the steering wheel and tore off a hunk for himself. His first language was Massango. He and Jenny seemed at ease with each other in French. I had only a few words of French, was quite in my daughter's keeping, and had no idea of the etiquette now. Did he assume we would help ourselves if we were hungry? Did he assume that were we hungry, we'd have had sense enough to buy our own baguette? Jenny had faced a lot by now but probably not exactly this. Besides, ill as she was, she wasn't hungry. Meanwhile, we pitched and rocked over deeply rutted red dirt roads. After eating three hunks of bread, the driver wrapped the paper around the remainder of his loaf and slid it to his left on the dash.

We were heading into hilly, half mountainous rainforests, as over the back roads of West Virginia though covered with mango trees, bamboo breaks, bananas, and ferns. More trees than I could possibly learn. One, a parasol tree, sent up sprays of long, graceful, silvery wands topped with clusters of twenty tongues. At least I guessed twenty. Every time I would fix on one to count, we'd rocket beneath it before I could work my way around its circle. Several times I eyed a quadrant, counted that, and multiplied. Twenty tongues. A kudzu-like vine covered much else. All along the road, red dust dimmed the green. The road itself dipped and curved and rose again with the driver straddling the ruts left from the last rainy season. In a few places, logs laid like a close-packed cattle guard shored up a washed-out piece of road. In the front seat, I jerked and pitched enough. Ten days later I would learn how it was to try to stay seated on a wheel cover in the back. Every now and then we'd pass a few wattle huts, thatched roofs over clay bricks packed between runners of bamboo. Some Jenny named as villages. They hardly seemed a crossroads. A hunter's game-of-the-day might hang near the road, a porcupine, monkey, antelope, or gazelle left dangling on a stake, its feet lashed with a cord. If we stopped, someone would come out of a house to bargain. Our driver bought two porcupines and a gazelle. We decided against a monkey though we took a long look. I noticed that Jenny, expert mall shopper that she once had been, could run her hand along the monkey's back and grip its hip and upper leg before deciding not to buy.

The next morning, with Jenny still weak from the flu, I ventured out for bread. All the town would know who I was by now and could figure out what I wanted. The baker nearest Jenny's house, a Malian known to sell out early, worked with an assistant before a large stone oven in a tin-roofed shanty behind his house. Almost two dozen neighborhood children and a few adults were gathered in the dark interior as I made my way inside to watch nine trays of new dough, each with five or six hand-span-long loaves, go into the oven. The baker splashed water on top of his loaves, flicking that from an old coffee can, then his assistant opened the oven door, drew out fresh bread from over the glowing coals, and inserted the new trays. Here we all were, facing warmly, and mostly in silence, the glow of the hearth and the magic of bread. Crowded shoulder to shoulder before his fire, we might all have sought shelter from a storm. Some of the children brought baskets, or a cloth, or a strip of paper in which to carry home the hot, new loaves. I bought six at about twelve cents each but had come barehanded. The baker sent a child to fetch a piece of paper bag for me. *Bonjour. Ça va. D'accord.* I took the bread and headed back to Jenny.

"Would you let your daughter marry an African," Guy had asked that first night at the discos. He was a tall, glisteningly black student from Libreville. He hoped to go further in computer training than could easily happen in Gabon. Perhaps he would go to the Ivory Coast or Senegal. With us also was Thomas, a gendarme and the owner of one of Mimongo's three disco-bars. Then Monica, and Alato, the other English teacher in Jenny's school. Alato comes from Ghana, where they speak English as they speak French in most of West-Central Africa; he came to translate and because he was interested.

We sat on benches, our backs to a block wall. We had started at Gabo-prix, the government-sponsored all-purpose store that stocked beer, canned goods, soap, motor oil, machetes, and Scotch. We had moved on to Thomas's bar and, after a round of drinks, had moved to another. We had sampled palm wine, not a drink I savored, and had changed to Regab, 16 oz. bottles of good beer, though seldom cold, and more or less the national drink of Gabon. Soon we would be off to the third disco. A strobe light at the far end of the hall picked up the beat of the music.

Thomas, with a round, glowing face and a little shorter than I, asked me to dance. At least that seemed to be what he invited. I held back as he turned to the floor, but followed warily and needn't have been alarmed. Most of the dancing was of individuals clumped loosely together. After a bit, the cluster reformed as a circle with one person after another venturing to the center. In returning to the circle, the soloist would select the next dancer by stepping up in front of him or her, asking to switch places. It's as if the music were the oven and in dancing we turned out the bread. Soon I was bidden. I jumped into the center, negotiated a dip and a turn or two, and stepped back. Everyone seemed accepting of what little I'd offered. With the rainy season over, they had been talking about its being winter in these equatorial highlands, and nearly everyone wore a sweater or jacket. I was in shirtsleeves and lightly covered with sweat.

To Guy's question I said, "Of course, if she wants to," hoping a simple answer would seem as guileless as my dancing. But his second question was more pressing: would these men be as welcome in my land as I was being made in theirs? Everywhere I had gone I had been introduced as *le papa de Jenny*, and since white faces are few in Mimongo, few introductions were needed. *"Le papa de Jenny,"* someone would declaim rather than ask on the street. I'd smile and add *bon soir*. Sometimes *ça va*. "You must send your daughter first," I replied, not so guileless after all, "Give her a two year head start, then go visit. It will work best, if she goes to a small town like Mimongo. Can you imagine my being welcomed in Libreville had I come with no relations, no friends, no French, and no job?"

"But are you being sincere when you say Jenny could marry an African?" Guy continued. I thought it a fair question though surprisingly direct. Americans are thought insincere, I was to learn, because we tend to be tactful, as I realized I was being. Such cautiousness, or attempts at empathy to cast a better light on them, often obscure our thought, so the Africans have a point. Could I really have answered his earlier question by asking, "When have the colonized ever been made welcome in the homes of the colonizers?"

Later I equivocated equally with Jenny's students who asked what Americans thought of Gabon—for which the best answer would probably have been, "Nothing"—and then what would their biggest problem be if they went to America? I said their biggest problem would be their tentative English. I could not bring myself to say what some must already have known, that they were poor and black. Now I welcomed the personal turn Guy had taken and said, "I think your question calls for a cigarette."

"We want to marry Jenny." Thomas took up their theme while fishing for a cigarette. "We all love her." I found his "we" more troubling than his invitation to dance. "We want to see her walking our roads with a wicker basket on her back, loaded with firewood." He mimed the tumpline that would ease her burden, but not mine, and he knew it. I had seen women walking alongside the road with *paniers* on their backs, carrying plantain, manioc, or firewood. Those scenes gave me some idea of local notions of marriage, which all these men knew would not square with mine. Thomas was married and was laughing at me, but for all I knew, he was planning ahead. I slid away from his question, too, by saying something about a father's natural concern when his daughter chooses to marry outside family traditions, that I would raise questions about that, but that the choice, finally, would be hers: for that's how it is, especially with a young woman in her mid-twenties in our culture.

Only after the appearance of the turbaned young woman at my bedside did I suspect the disco may have been a way of avoiding the *bwiti,* the strobe lights and African rock a way of shutting out the masks and their mysteries. Maybe it was best to be home before the dance released whatever it would. The next night I played solitaire until two thirty. Several more nights would pass before I slept easily. Dorothee came to mind often. Could her youthful energy have led to such adventuring? Or was I dreaming of Jenny and facing some fear that I was losing her to Africa? The appearance I remember took bodily form and glided from my room without touching the floor. Could I call that a dream? And why, if I could, did I still search local faces, seeking another answer?

Here was a crisis, though I was slow to face it. My visitor was more than I had known in my half century of the experience of night. Most of my understanding told me to forget it—it was but a dream—and to pay attention to the day. I might at most regard it as one more traveler's tale, such as the shock of seeing the Parthenon on the Acropolis in Athens, dead on, at eye level, and noting the seventeen columns that define its wholly standing and perfect seeming north side. How did they arrive at seventeen,

I remember wondering, much as I wondered at how Jenny had learned to feel the monkey's haunch before deciding not to buy. Remarkable that view, wholly extraordinary, like finding a pink bear on the streets of Chicago. But on second thought, very little remains extraordinary; we recover from being startled and go on to our next business. Where can we change some money, find our next cappuccino, or glass of wine?

I had found myself in an international community deep in the equatorial forests of Africa. It centered on the secondary school in which Jenny taught. The math teacher and his wife were from Mali. The French teacher was from Guinea. The science teacher came from Benin and owned a cab in the Congo, in Pointe Noir. Alato, the English teacher from Ghana, was married to a woman from Togo. The principal, a Gabonese, had studied in Philadelphia, Jenny's adoptive home before the Peace Corps. On his wall he had a souvenir banner from Hannibal, Missouri, which was little over one hundred miles east of my hometown and only a little farther south from the Iowa town where I now lived and from which Jenny went off to college. The Spanish teacher, also Gabonese, had studied in Salamanca and Madrid. A few days before, I had flown in from Valencia. He and I spoke Spanish together as I did with a Peace Corps staff member in Libreville who came from Equatorial Guinea, a former Spanish colony.

A number of the merchants were Muslims from Mali. Another was from Mauritania. During the Gulf War, townspeople had watched closely to see whether Jenny would buy from them and how they would treat her. She stood at ease within their shops, conversing with them, and they remained welcoming, distant war proving small impediment to the sparkle of a young woman, or to commerce. But neighbors had paused in the street near those shops when Jenny walked inside and sometimes moved into the doorways to watch and listen.

This variety of nations was superimposed on an even thicker variety of languages, first, or at least most broadly, the nearly universal French, then Massango, Fang, Mitshogo, Bandjabi, Bambara, Yoruba, and Ewe. The first four of those could be heard in Gabon alone. Ewe in Ghana (with English) and in Togo and Benin. Yoruba in Benin and Nigeria. Bambara in Guinea and Mali. I never met anyone monolingual, and though I have found occasion to suspect otherwise, I generally find it impossible to believe that a bilingual person can be a fool. Even the cleaning woman at Jenny's school spoke French and one or two African languages. "How many languages do you know?" was the first question children in Jenny's class asked me. "One and a half," I answered, though that was a stretch. I had studied several, but Spanish was the only language other than English that I came close to speaking. At parties in Spain, I tried always to face whatever speaker and concentrate hard on what was said.

Jenny, though, caught things behind her back and overlapping conversations on all sides. "They're talking about whether Peace Corps volunteers get paid," she told me in a café in Libreville about the conversation at a table behind her, and toward which she had not even glanced. She was quick to answer students in the back of the room who thought they had not been overheard, or at least understood, and in their French at that. On the street, she seemed at home with everyone.

A couple of days later we went to visit Jeannette. Much of the daily routine in Mimongo is to drop in on friends. Not a whole lot need be said; absence is the burden, not silence. So we sat with Jeannette in her outdoor kitchen under palm thatch while she and Jenny absorbed the calm of the day, gossiped a little, and while Jeannette tended the fire and fried chicken and plantain. She arranged her wood like spokes on a wheel, the fire glowing at its hub, with a few rocks centered to support the pan and with others forming an incomplete outer ring, reflecting heat inward. Several chickens in their original state almost walked into the fire. Occasionally, from my side of the fire, I would do as she and push a spoke closer to the center. Jeannette would acknowledge my small help with a smile. I admired her deft way of peeling the tough, green plantain. She used the back part of a butcher knife, controlling it with the palm of her right hand, breaking into the peel sharply and chipping the whole of it away in three or four pieces as she rocked her knife on the cutting board. I wondered how long it would take to master the same strokes and to keep my left, guiding fingers out from under the blade. I was attracted, even mesmerized by the fire, but we left while I still tried to penetrate the mystery of Jeannette's dark, round face, and to weigh her identity against Dorothee's as my possible visitation.

"It is easier for an African to know the West than for you to know us," Salami said the next afternoon. I did not dispute that; the colonized is usually the better observer. Salami was the science teacher from Benin, the one who also owned a cab in Pointe Noir, thus gaining a little leverage on his hopes of building a home in his own country. We were sitting late into the sunset on side-turned beer crates propped against the west wall of Gabo-prix, drinking Regab once more. Jenny and Salami spoke easily, and most of their conversation I just watched. Now and then a remark of Salami's seemed aimed at me, and the pace would slow to allow for translations. He wanted to provoke me, he said.

"A ghost" was his confident answer about my visitor; "it was a ghost." Then after a half a moment of silence, "But you won't let yourself believe in ghosts, will you?"

I remembered my first year in college when an instructor in the required writing course asked whether we believed in ghosts, and of what we made, over the next few assignments, of our adamant denial. I almost found myself replying to Salami that what he took to be a ghost we would take to be a dream, which would only have meant admitting that, no, I could not believe in a ghost, and condescending to him as well. So I admired instead the shrewd insight of his remark. It had been to the point and had also triggered a moment of *déjà vu*, summoning my wonder, as a freshman, that "apparition," "presentiment," "hallucination," or "dream" were all acceptable references to experience, when "ghost" had not been. Had Salami said *revenant*, rather than *spectre*, would that have eased the mystery?

Since Jenny was about to leave Mimongo, she was preparing to give some parties, the first for her "family," that had looked after her and Monica so well. That was a family of women and children. Its heads of household were Maman Mabe, who had ten children of her own, several still with her, along with various grandchildren. Her sister, Maman Koumba, was her partner in homemaking. I don't know how many children Maman Koumba had. Monica had spoken to the two of them on the road early in her time in Mimongo, had asked about the farm and whether she could walk along with them and see it. She could, but they made her sit in the shade and rest after a ten-kilometer hike into the hills while they cultivated small crops of manioc and bananas. By way of this trip, Monica and Jenny were adopted, told to consider the Mamans' family theirs. Later the Mamans gave Jenny a *panier*, one of those wicker baskets Thomas had mentioned; and I have a picture of her wearing it strapped to her back while she crosses a vine bridge. She had spent a lot of time in the kitchen with Maman Mabe, Dorothee, Jeannette, and other women. Dorothee, who had asked to dance with me, was a daughter of one of the Mamans.

"Are you an African father or Jenny's real one," Maman Mabe asked in the same conversation that revealed that she had ten children to my two and was ten years younger than I. Out of ties of friendship and community, an African father could have many children not biologically his own. In the short time I was there, we spent an evening with the Mamans and their family, the small house well swept out, and its walls washed down, dining and drinking palm wine and Regab; and they spent a night with us, in a house less immaculately kept, for what is dirt to an African is not necessarily alarming to young American women.

Jenny had just received a letter from a Gabonese friend of the year before, a young woman now attending college in the States and working that summer at Jenny's old French Camp in Minnesota. She was alarmed by the squalor of the Minnesota lakes, the sand and dirt tracked into the cabins, the awful creepy crawly things and, worst of all, the huge mosquitoes. One might guess from her letter that she was less comfortable with mosquitoes than with ghosts. And perhaps that's not so strange. Alato was to tell me that malaria is the most feared killer of children in Africa.

The next day, at Jenny and Monica's larger party, Alato took it upon himself to move us from eating to dancing. Salami had brought his music system, various friends had contributed tapes, and Alato, graceful and charming, took possession of the floor to designate different couples to "lead us into the dance." Jenny and I were called upon first, and soon most of us were up and moving. I danced with Dorothee, with the young and very pregnant wife of the manager of the electric company, with the young and very pregnant wife of Gabo-prix's *concessionaire,* she being also Jenny's prize student. When I wasn't dancing with either, they were dancing together, each using a hand to support her stomach. And I danced with the bilingual cleaning woman.

A young man no one seemed to know had appeared on the porch early in the afternoon, just waiting. His shirttail hung out of his pants; he wore a baseball cap, dirty gray chinos, and thong sandles. Eventually Jenny offered him a beer, and he later took a place on the floor that he held for hours. He was the most at ease dancer of us all, but something was wrong for no one would consent to dance with him. He seldom asked, seeming content to be around people and the music. But once in a while, he invited one or another of the women, who would shrug him off even though his rhythm seemed infallible. As the evening wore on, he found it possible to ask for another beer. It seemed likely that news of Jenny's party had spread out to several of the smaller villages and that this young man, perhaps a former student at the school, had walked in for it. His feet, thonged and dusty, were as confident as wire brushes on a drum as he held the floor.

At one quiet moment, I sat talking with Alato. His eyes glittered with both seriousness and good humor. He was telling me of the Pygmies, one of the Bantu people, forest people, many of whom live near Mimongo and are unlikely to be seen unless they wish it. Such is the lore. They move through the forest without breaking a twig. They are like fairy versions of Natty Bumppo and the Mohicans, of all the Native American imagery I had clung to as a boy. I had already asked Salami what one or two people he thought most essentially African, knowing I asked an impossible question. What one state best represents the United States? He came close: the Yoruba, his own people, and the Pygmies, the people of the forest. Alato was enthusiastic about them, too, and about how I should study the Pygmies should I really want to know Africa. He had learned a lot about them himself. "How," I asked.

"From a video."

"A video?"

"Yes, made by an American anthropologist." I could rent it.

The teachers had all been together at their principal's house the night before. There we sat along the walls, perhaps in a style inherited from village chiefs in their lodges. Jenny and I held places of honor, in the middle of the wall facing the door. Her principal addressed us in a lengthy speech, delivered first in English for my benefit. He spoke about Jenny's dedicated work at the school and how they will miss her. He spoke of how, when she came to Mimongo, she had gone out from her house and seized the initiative to meet local people. He mentioned how she had taken her own clothes to the river to wash, joining the neighborhood women there, and how she had kept her own shoes clean, as other villagers took pride in doing, even through the rainy season. I noticed that the principal chose not to complicate matters by mentioning when Jenny, like the other teachers, none of them locals, stopped going to the river but employed a villager instead. Finally, he honored me as the parent of such a child.

At Jenny's party, Alato remembered the part of the parent being honored by the work of the child and thought it a worthy aspiration. His principal had spoken well for him. I in turn had stood and spoken for our family, dragging Jenny to the floor to translate. I thanked them all and spoke of Jenny's mother who would have loved to have made this trip. I hoped that some of their children or children from their school would one day find their way to my country, perhaps to my university, where I might prove an African father for them as they had been for Monica and Jenny. I do not remember more of what I said, but I did not challenge the principal's length of address, or his bilingual fluency, and sat down as quickly as I thought decent. I thought I had done well, but Alato's memory of his principal's speech suggested that I had failed to rise to the occasion, extended eloquence being, I suspect, of greater importance in African tradition than in our own.

A VCR had provided the other entertainment at the principal's. First a series of short rube-in-the-city sketches from Cameroon. The rube can't find his way across a street; he mistakes the number on a bus for the hour at which it departs; he doesn't know how to behave in a restaurant. When the meal heats him up, he takes off his shirt and towels off his underarms. Then he's stuck with the bill and is led to the kitchen. Most of the guests kept a laughing eye on this action while chatting with the persons seated nearest to them.

Suddenly taped highlights from MTV filled the screen. After Michael Jackson, Madonna, and Ice-T, I came face to face with Bob James, a jazz pianist and high school classmate and friend. I hadn't seen him in over thirty years, but there he was, graying, bearded and unmistakable, leading a quartet called Fourplay. For a moment he seemed to be staring at me, with a hint of the interested expression of the ghost. I remembered an afternoon, after a year or two of college. Bob and I had been playing tennis, and coming off the court, he turned to me and said, "You'd probably play better if you looked less as if you were watching yourself trying to do it right." Now all these years later, in the highlands of Gabon, my first memory of a moment with Bob ran right to the sting of my awkward self-consciousness, and to a sense of his accurate knowing. Though I could explain the technology of his appearance easily enough, it was shocking to face him in those equatorial forests. But maybe that is what travel comes down to. We run across one thing after another that we have no reason to expect until each appearance, prospect, sight, even ghost, seems but one more remarkable, though manageable experience. Taking a snap shot, we move on.

A couple of nights later, the grade school celebrated the end of its year by offering most of Mimongo a party. It was their Fair. All the children and young adolescents went there, and for most that was the end of their formal education. A large crowd had gathered as Monica, Jenny, and I were ushered to seats midway down the longest wall. The principal, a tall, vigorous man in a clay-colored suit with a white shirt and open collar, made a welcoming speech that understated what was to follow. He referred to their small hospitality and made it seem that we would be eating sandwiches. But as he was speaking, the table began to fill with porcupine, plantain, gazelle, turkey, chicken, manioc, taro, monkey—its skull was in the pot—French fries, antelope, and rice.

The principal invited the town prefect to lead the way. He in turn deferred to the women. Soon a representative of the school took over, going around and motioning to each of us when she thought our turn had come. There was a very clear order, within which we were flattered. As everyone in the main room returned to their places with a full plate, more people were let in from outside. Apparently two or three other rooms had filled with visitors, and food was offered until the buffet was cleared. Meanwhile, the principal kept showing where to place things on the table, moving dishes around to find an order that pleased him. He sent students and staff to bring more food, to pour beer and palm wine. He went among the guests in line, urging them to fill their plates. I found I liked the antelope, or was it gazelle, and I didn't mind the porcupine. But I left brother monkey staring at me in his pot.

As dinner ended, we were ushered onto a bare, earthen tract alongside the schoolhouse, where a huge bonfire had been readied. The logs were the size of railroad ties and leaned together in tepee fashion. People milled around them. Soon young men carried out chairs and couches from the hall where we had been dining and set them in rows along either side of the fire. The prefect was shown to a center seat on one side and we were led to a place opposite him. I could see Thomas finding a seat on the far side and someone said he had a gift for me. I smiled and waved. By then the entertainment was beginning. The principal lit the bonfire that flared as if rigged for a disaster movie and introduced what was to follow—poetry readings, skits, dances.

The readings proved to be recitations by young male students. They were declamatory, excessive, full of verve, and comic. The shortest speaker was the crowd favorite. The poetry was in French and was followed closely, with laughter, cheering, occasional boos or hisses. They seemed like parlor poems of our last century—"Horatio at the Bridge," "The Cremation of Sam McGee," "Gunga Din"—and the bolder the readings, the stronger the approval. The short, young favorite among the readers might be a prefect or principal in the making.

In the skits, too, male characters dominated. The favorite reader later played a suitor, one of several, the poorest, who borrowed all his clothing and accouterments from his rivals and won the hand of his lady, only to be defrocked, literally, as all his lenders reclaimed their possessions, and his bride abandoned him.

Another skit was on colonialism and linguistic advantage. A hustler, proficient in Mitshogo and French, accompanies a group of colonial governors to a village and interprets them to the village elders: "We are the Plenipotentiaries of Whatsabiggoosa," proclaim the governors. "These are the colonialist thugs from the coast," explains their translator while the governors nod and smile.

"We have come to make known to you the benefits of Civilization." Or as the translator puts it, "They have come here to throw their weight around because their wives want them out of town for a while."

"Of course we expect that you will honor us with a banquet." Or, "Throw a few scrawny monkeys on the fire and we'll tell them it's antelope." Each translation brought roars of approval until the French officials departed well satisfied. Meanwhile we sat across from the prefect who smiled at us in calm good humor.

Whereas the oratory and the declamations had been performed by the young men, the dancers were young women. They performed dance after dance in small groups with varying makeup and costuming. Sometimes they wore whiteface. Sometimes short skirts of banana leaves that rippled to accentuate their hips. If the young men were being vetted for their place in this society, the young women were being tested similarly for a role that could not be made clearer.

Though dances varied, their format was similar—a line of dancers filed in from beyond the fire, one short step then another forward, each step extending a line of motion perpendicular to the main action, which was the girls swinging their hips like puppies shaking water from their skin. All the while they made a steady, incremental advance across the yard. Here I saw the origin of the circle dance at the discos, for always, when the line had advanced as far as possible, it paused while one girl after another stepped forward to take a turn, like a jazz troupe running through its soloists. The men let us know who had impressed them most.

Among the dancers were two girls I had seen only that afternoon helping Jenny clean up after her party. In Jenny's house, they had the manner of pre-teens. They were slender, just beginning to mature, as supple as the silvery wands of the parasol tree, and as shy as if they wished to hold its spray of twenty leaves before their faces. They giggled in the kitchen, took several tubs of dishes down to the river to wash, then swept and washed the floor. When they were through, Jenny asked if they would prefer money or to select from a cache of trinkets she had for such purposes. Her grandmother kept sending her crayons, balloons, baseball cards, whistles, pins, and other such things that Jenny might use as prizes in her classes. She still had a box of cheap loot as she was ending her second year, and to the girls it seemed like Halloween. They were quick to indicate the box, bent straight over from the waist to sift through it on the floor, whispered about options, and took away three items each.

Since we were to leave in the morning, we resisted a last night of drinking with Thomas. He did offer his present, however, four cup-shaped baskets woven together like a clover. Again he said something about marrying Jenny, and I wondered whether I should construe the basket as a bridal payment. That was only one of several questions left unanswered. I never knew what those girls thought of being girls with Jenny one afternoon and targets of male desire that very evening, how eager or victimized they may have felt, or whether only I was unnerved. I never knew how Dorothee or Jeannette luxuriated and suffered under the gaze of the men they knew, and who came to know them, and left them with children. Neither could I gauge the degree of irony that might attend Alato's sense of learning about his forest neighbors from the videos of anthropologists, or about his recommending those videos to me. Nor did I gauge on the part of the women who danced with me, especially the young, pregnant-again mothers, the spectacle I might be offering them.

Nor, of course, did I ever understand the ghost. Even now, there are nights when I try to believe that I have actually beheld one. To believe that would be an extraordinary thing, like seeing a pink bear in a city. Or like seeing through to the other side of reality and watching myself change my mind by turning it inside out. But perhaps for Alato and his friends looking down into the dust of the road outside the last disco of Mimongo, perhaps for Salami as he found himself quite capable of reading me, perhaps for Jeannette tending her fire or for Dorothee rising to dance, it is no more unusual than having Jennys and Monicas come among them and finding themselves hosting Jenny's dad. Though I had managed to make it to Mimongo and witness an important stage in Jenny's life, I had penetrated nothing at all of Africa. Perhaps that turbaned woman had just turned away from me, when she found me unable to accept her, and in disdain had departed.

On our way out of town, we passed Maman Mabe on the road and our driver stopped so she and Jenny could hug each other. I believe Maman Mabe made a point of being on that road at that early hour, for out of the *panier* on her back she drew a small bottle filled with a green potion, a last gift for Jenny. We were off to Libreville, the big city, where there were bad people, and this potion, when rubbed on, would render her invisible to all who meant her harm.

AFTER WORDS: This would be the end of my story, but not of Jenny's. She spent the next year in Libreville, moving from the field to Peace Corps administration. Her last official act was to escort six new volunteers to their posts in the interior. Hers are the "After Words" as she wrote home, reporting on having escorted the new Peace Corps members to Mouila and Mimongo:

"We flew from Libreville to Mouila," she wrote. "I got to watch all their faces as they realized we were landing on a dirt runway and that there wasn't really any airport building to speak of. Even though Mouila was not my post there were several people I knew at the airport, either traveling themselves or meeting people. With a little finagling I was able to find someone with a truck to transport all our things to one of the houses. The next morning the two for Mimongo and I took off up into the mountains. I spent three and a half days helping them settle in and seeing my friends. I had forgotten how many little things are hard in the beginning. Things like how to collect rain water, how to put together a water filter, how to mop a floor without a mop, how to cut and clean a chicken.

"I got to see Jeannette's new baby boy and sit around and play with the kids at the Mamans' house. One afternoon was particularly fun. It was late afternoon and the two Mamans had just gotten back from their plantation in the forest and were exhausted. So we were sitting there doing nothing but talking about how difficult life is. As we were talking other women started showing up, ones I knew by face, but not by name. Soon there were probably twenty women and girls in the family's yard. Maman Koumba suddenly started organizing all of them for something, although I couldn't figure out what since they were going on and on in Mitshogo. Finally one of the older girls explained to me that the President of Gabon was coming to Mimongo next Tuesday and that these women were organizing the songs and dances they would perform for him in hopes of being given envelopes of money for their loyalty to his party.

"So they started to sing and dance, teaching the younger girls words and showing them which way to move their hips to which rhythms. It was so lively and so relaxed. I had seen a million traditional dances and this was essentially the same music and dance, but no costumes and ceremony. They were just having fun. I don't remember ever having seen so much laughter. After watching for a good fifteen minutes I decided this was my chance to try to learn those dances. After all they were just practicing. So, I kicked off my shoes and placed myself next to the older girls and followed along the best I could. Without even realizing it I started to sing and move right along with them. What a blast. And the best part was that not one of them even batted an eye. It was as if they had always expected me to join right in. We danced until the little children sitting in the kitchen started wailing for food and all the women dispersed to their homes. I, too, put my shoes back on, said good-night and headed home to the two new Americans and our spaghetti dinner. All I could think of was how the best moments are always spontaneous. You never have your camera, and no one but yourself will ever really know that moment of your life.

"The next morning we were awakened by two of the boys in the family. Maman Mabe had sent them down with a live chicken. Their message was 'Maman says to tell Jenny to feed the guests properly.' I guess it was their welcome gesture to the new Americans, but it also reminded me of any mother anywhere worrying that her daughter was not following protocol or was just generally slacking off in politeness. We accepted the chicken, found someone else to kill it, and ate like kings and queens.

"So, as I said, I spent three good days in Mimongo. I got to say goodbye to everyone important to me and pass on my last words of wisdom to my successors. Then I hopped into the back of a pickup truck and pulled out of town. The family had gathered to say goodbye, but the truck that was coming to get me was late, so the Mamans had to leave, before I actually left. They gave me a basket they had made for me which is quite beautiful. We all cried and promised to write. But it just seems so final. Of course in true Peace Corps melodramatic form we passed both Mamans on the road. So they ran after the truck and we waved and screamed at each other. They saying, '*Mwana wami akea*! (my child is leaving)' and me, '*Mono, na kea* (Big Sister, I am leaving).'"

Letter to Jix, or Writing From the Inside Out

It's not easy to write of Richard (Jix) Lloyd-Jones, who chaired our department nine of my first ten years here. Not only was Jix a mysterious man, but, through many years as his colleague, we were in key ways opposites. Nevertheless, we had two things in common. Jix had damaged lungs and I asthma, so when he paused on a landing of EPB, wheezing, I knew the feeling well. Inhalers kept mine at bay. Jix was less fortunate. He had worse than severe asthma always and stopped at every landing. Also we were both closet poets.

Then I appeared suddenly, by desperate chance, as a possible replacement for his closest colleague and friend, Richard Braddock. That must have been disorienting though I was blithely ignorant of it. For years those two collaborated on, and eventually published, *Research in Written Composition*, brought out while I was in graduate school. They were way ahead of whatever game I had, and suddenly Braddock was gone, killed in a traffic accident while on sabbatical in Australia. Otherwise I wouldn't have been invited to speak to the English Department at Iowa and be considered for a position. I came armed only with what I knew, which had nothing of research about it. But I could draw on my experience, such as it was, in April of 1975. I can imagine Jix listening to much I had to say that afternoon and thinking, "That is not what I meant at all." Nevertheless he assented, and a couple of years later—he was Chair by then—he assented as well—it may even have been his idea—to my taking over *The Iowa Review*.

I'd been given no assignment for my talk. But I knew the position was to teach writing, so I described my experience as a teacher and writer. And I spoke at length of the writing course I took during my first year at Amherst College, which then was still an all men's college and very much aware of being a customary next step—though it was hardly that for me—after Deerfield, Andover, or Choate.

"List six principles by which you live," we were asked our first day, and we all did, surprised though some of us were, that we could summon so many. The next day we learned that all but one of us had declared himself "an individualist." Well, then, was the one fellow who hadn't thought of that our only original thinker? What does it mean to be an individual, anyway? Write an essay about that.

Or, later, do you believe in ghosts? Of course not, we chorused, each of us in a page or two of prose. Who do you think we are, superstitious fools? Then we received several reports of encounters with the supernatural: apparitions, hallucinations, presences, even ghosts. Well, do you believe in ghosts now? And we all bent to qualify our first position. The next step was to observe that most of us had changed our minds and to ask what it means to do that. What happens when you change your mind? How does that occur? Do you change all or just some of it?

But the assignments, the writing prompts, were considerably more cunning than I have suggested. Here are the first three:

> 1. A great American poet is quoted in a recent book as having denounced college teaching that "frisks Freshmen of their principles." Think about the problem seriously for a time and then set down a list of a half dozen of your principles (one or two thoughtful sentences for each), and

explain in a paragraph your interest in retaining them. (Note: keep a legible copy of your principles.)

2. When examined, this metaphor of "frisking" has its interest, has it not. Rightly or wrongly you are being taken into custody, accused perhaps, your principles are your weapons, you may or may not choose to produce them with a show of violence, they provide a defense, etc. Or you are at the racetrack and your wallet is picked. Consider for a moment your principles as weapons of self defense (and of aggression), and write a page telling why in a civilized community of lawns and books you need to be able to defend yourself. Who is your enemy? With what does he threaten you?

3. Leaf through the college catalogue with your principles in mind. Find a course that looks as though it might have the effect of despoiling you of a principle. Quote the principle involved and the course description; then write a page—it will be imaginative writing of course—telling how you think this effect might be obtained. Short of avoiding the course, how would you go about defending yourself?

Not only did that course keep me off balance, it seemed always to strive for the ineffable and to demand we write of matters we had not considered. Note that parenthetical clause about imaginative writing; almost off-handedly, we were being asked to invent. Furthermore, the assignments reward close reading that few of us were capable of. Who, I wonder, and it certainly was not I, challenged right off that first metaphor, "frisk," which came as you may already know, from Robert Frost? I'm sure the few who did, were there any, were well rewarded by the instructor's taking a close interest in what they said. And what to make too of the assumed adversarial relation? We may not have warred with our instructors, the dozen or so, each one shepherding about twenty of us through these assignments, but we were soon aware of being on guard against the next probing question. Scholarship was beside the point. These were personal questions that challenged us to answer as ourselves. I doubt that plagiarism ever occurred to any of us. That course made me live for an entire school year as an earnest commentator on my own experience, that is, as a writer. It has had the most lasting influence on me of any course whatsoever.

We did not learn formal structures of argument, or even of paragraphing. We had no handbook. We learned to invent, with caution, reflection, and qualification, while assessing our commitment to whatever we thought. Or maybe I could say, to what we thought we thought, as we found all our clichés challenged. Hadn't we rendered "individualist" a cliché already, right off the bat? Soon we discovered that metaphor devoid of literal meaning is suspect. As in changing one's mind, "Is that like changing your shirt? Changing a tire? Or is it more like changing a habit?"

I have heard that the aim of that course was for us to compose our intellectual autobiographies by way of about eighty short compositions sequenced through a school year, three a week the first semester, and two a week the second. Each year gave birth to a new sequence composed by our instructors. "Now I've got you out in the open where I can get at you," an instructor wrote on a paper soon passed around among that writer's friends, which prompted, among those friends, questions such as, were we the writer, would we want to be got at and was that like being frisked? Meanwhile, in class, dittoed excerpts from our writings were our reading, a fresh set each day, taken from the papers just handed back; and we walked the tightrope always of hoping to be quoted and wary of what our instructor, and classmates, would find fault with if we were.

Surely both Jix and Carl Klaus took an interest in that part of my talk since I was reporting on a format they had come to value. They too were composing writing sequences. My college course, though I didn't know it at the time, had been a model for their work. Carl told me much later that he and Jix shared their sequences, leaving them typed in the other's mail slot, as if they were exchanging poems.

Meanwhile another factor was at play. The Iowa Institute on Writing, for directors of first year courses all across the nation, was being planned and would come to fruition four years later. Jix would lead a seminar on rhetorical theory, Carl one on assignment sequences in composition courses, and that left me, possibly, to lead one on writing across the curriculum of the liberal arts. We didn't have the phrasing yet, but it arose soon after, and our Institute had something to do with that. As I spoke, I was being vetted for that position, and my first year course made an impression on both Carl and Jix.

In fact they found its influence a little shocking as I plunged ahead in the only way I knew, to make it up as I went along, as I had all through that first year; to construct my own "momentary stays against confusion" as Frost defined his poems, and look to no handbook. For the next three years, I experimented with a course I called Writing Science. Not Writing in the Sciences, but Writing Science itself. Right off I discovered that students bringing in work from chemistry, physics, psychology, or whatever other discipline, had a hard time reading each other. Each writer was too far into his or her own specialization, and it doesn't take many steps in before you have shut the door behind you. About that time, I came upon a text called *Seeing and Writing*, by Walker Gibson who had been an instructor at Amherst. He had moved on, but he had taken its first principle with him: challenge writers to invent before you worry about shaping their inventions.

My favorite example from his book was "Reading the Wind," that is building an anemometer and describing the wind it reveals to you. Now, assuming you are willing to try, you can come up with hundreds of possibilities without running out to the nearest airport and copying theirs. Moreover, you can revise and improve your anemometer and share your work with collaborators who may help improve it further, which is a lot like the work of science. Open a bundle of newspapers on the sidewalk and describe how they blow away. Dangle a paper cup with colored water over a white sheet pegged to the ground; punch a whole in the cup and describe the pattern the water makes on the sheet. Set a series of bottles of water in a row, filled to different levels, and write the music you hear the wind play over them. And in each case, try to define the wind you discover. Is the wind writing its face on the sheet the same as that whistling over bottles?

I came to call this not science but a serious parody of science and worked out possibilities for adjacent disciplines. Go out on a winter night and describe movement you find in the stars. Attend a regional girls basketball tournament—it was still six-girl, half-court basketball—and write an ethnography of what you observe. Go to an exhibition of unfamiliar art—African masks and pots was one opportunity—and sketch several classifications. These assignments carried over to our Institute. In one planning session, I was describing them to Jix and Carl. They were a little taken aback. In spite of their commitment to invention-first sequences, they still seemed to hope I had a helpful handbook of rules in me somewhere, a dependable structure, or series of modulated structures, that would smooth the way for writing in the sciences, the social sciences, and humanities. But out of ignorance and habit, I had no such thing, and now they were stuck with me. Finally, I think it was Carl who turned to me and said, "Oh, I get it. You're working from the inside out." I had never put it like that, from the inside out, rather, I suppose, than from the outside in, but I quickly said, "Yes" and tried to live up to claims an old course had laid on me. Jix, with his calm, Olympian tolerance, just smiled.

Now I can add what I didn't know enough to say that first afternoon in Iowa since I had not yet been surprised by it. All semester long, my first term at Amherst, not a single passage was chosen from my work as an example, good or bad, for my fellow students. Our last essay was to serve as our exam. It was to be a couple of pages longer and, for the first time, addressed no particular question. I was on my own.

I wrote of work one summer during high school when I signed on to pour cement atop a series of grain elevators rising over the rooftops and shade trees of our midwestern, county seat town. Once the pouring started, crews were needed around the clock, and I joined the night crew, from eleven to seven. Meditative, soul-searching time, especially at seventeen, even if one does not think to say so. We rose to work by standing on the open rim of the big cement bucket, rising between the running cables that lifted it to the working deck. We kept our hands close to the cables for an illusory sense of safety. You couldn't cling to them, but their presence offered a frame within which you stood straight and balanced. The bucket rim was about as wide as a piece of railroad track. We stood a little sideways on it and so were hoisted a hundred feet or more off ground. Rising upward, we savored our daring and exposure. If I slipped, I'd try to fall into the cement, not to the ground. This was long before OSHA. Once on top, where flimsy board railings that served more as warnings than true restraints deterred our falling off, we stood level with our well lit, courthouse dome. There we sorted and placed steel reinforcing rods and pushed wheelbarrows of cement along plank runways over mesh-covered forms to wherever a new load was needed. Once my barrow lurched so that I stumbled toward a railing, and a co-worker, an older black man, caught my arm and steadied me. I won't say I would have plunged through the flimsy plank railing and fallen, but I might have. I remember seeing the ground beneath me for half a second before I caught myself, or he caught me, and I remember the smile we exchanged as he steadied me and I regained my footing.

A classmate already known to have served time in the state reform school was also on the job. One night he stood below, patting his windbreaker pocket, asking men if they wanted to see what he had. He said he had a gun. Eventually he rose up top on the bucket rim. But he never really got to work. The foreman wanted to see the gun and then wanted to take it. Marion wouldn't permit that so the foreman dismissed him on the spot. It's a persistent image, Marion standing with a few men atop of an adjacent tower, their voices accenting the shadowy, summer night, not angry but insistent. Then Marion turning and descending on the bucket's rim. He looked small enough once below, his shoulders hunched, striding off into the night. He never returned to school.

I've long since lost that essay but my instructor found in it, from me, for the first and only time, a note of my being out in the open, unfrisked, perhaps, and venturing exposure. A long swatch of it was the lone example he offered our class our last day. A classmate who had been in the same section as I surprised me by remembering my essay and reminding me of it at our fiftieth reunion. Now a physicist, he remembered detail, after fifty-four years, and so reminded me. He remembered because he felt he learned something: as he put it, writing could be indirect and be the better for it. He said that moment confirmed his scientific bent, just as my mediocrity in a required calculus-physics course tipped me in the opposite direction, which led, almost twenty years later, to Iowa.

Where, over a good many years, I gradually discovered something like a principle of writers and writing. Many writers, most perhaps, when tasked with writing as a task, begin looking for an exit almost as soon as they start. "How can I get out of here?" is their guiding question. Others, fewer, writers you don't really have to teach although you may be able to coach, take to the page wondering what they can do with it, how can they make that page, and the next one, open up? If you could give the first group of writers the advantage of the second, our problems would be solved. The assignment sequence I struggled with and those we invented later attack that problem. Insofar as they manage to engage the student as a person, that person, almost a writer, begins to sense within the self something as yet undiscovered. It's as if one is surprised by finding a forgotten item in a pocket that it would be best to take out and look at before that pocket gets picked. Looking at it and rubbing it up a bit leads to invention as invention summons an inventor.

If I could take this a step further, I would suggest that invention stems from seeing, intently. Quick leaps to what you think is there, without looking closely, almost always land on clichés. I am reminded of several writing texts from years ago. They liked to posit four kinds of writing: description, explanation, narration, and argument. Furthermore they organized those kinds as a hierarchy with description on the bottom, argument on top. Right off I scoffed at the suggestion that argument should outrank all the great narratives—whichever ones you care to name. But I realized too that the context was our preparation of first year students for future academic work, most of which would in fact privilege argument. It probably took me another decade, maybe two, to go further and focus on description as much more than just work to be got over quickly before the serious stuff. Fresh description is what matters. Writers who make that discovery work from new ground where they can be "got at." Maybe frisked. But that's where a writer's adventure begins.

All of this took us a long way and I had the privilege of teaching writing for years with Carl and Jix, with Paul Diehl, Susan Lohafer, Carol de St. Victor, Fred Woodard, Brooks Landon, Patricia Foster, Tom Simmons, Bonnie Sunstein, John

Harper, Robin Hemley and John D'Agata. First came the Institute of 1979-1981 and then the Nonfiction Writing Program that started earlier and has gone much further. Collectively, we went rather far with our efforts but not all the way. We never solved the problem of making a good writer of someone for whom the writing remains a task, or for whom—and it's usually the same writer—description relies on recitation of what is mostly known. The sequences Jix and Carl devised, like those that fixed my old college course in the memories of a generation of Amherst alumni, were one way of addressing the problem: invention first. That our Nonfiction Program has leaned more and more toward invention means that its applicants, and then participants, come to us having already discovered motives for writing that they can describe in detail. Thus they seduce us into sharing their interests. In effect they have made sequences of their own writing already. We find it hard to keep up.

At the Fair

"Book dust is the best aphrodisiac" a friend remarked when I told him of our librarian's lithe step behind dawning book ranges, and of her husky voice reciting, "The grave's a fine and private place, but none I think do there embrace, The grave's a fine and private place . . ." over and over as I kept pace with her behind shelf after shelf of old books before turning into her late afternoon path at an aisle. "Who wrote that?" she asked as we paused face to face, all but touching, and I dropped my gaze, mumbled "Marvell," and slipped past her into the dusk of prose and rhyme and prose.

In that same library where morning after morning I walked past that same librarian—think Aubrey Beardsley's Salome with henna in her hair—on my way to my carrel with its dissertation-in-progress on Old English poetry, *Beowulf* and that lot, and from which I often rose to wander narrow, book-lined aisles, one reason no doubt for my lasting fondness for secondhand bookstores, I came one afternoon into an opening at the end of a long dim aisle, almost a glade along a sunny wall where shelves displayed new arrivals and where I found a *North American Review* in its bold red cover with stark white lettering which I opened to find came from Mt. Vernon, Iowa, and I remember my knee-jerk, adopted, Eastern seaboard surprise: "How can they get away with that?" by which I meant speaking for North America from the vantage of an Iowa town. But I remember equally the thought that steadied me as I stumbled: Why not, what could be more North American? Didn't Mt. Vernon lie less than three hundred miles north by northeast of the town I called home? So curious my coming to live in a zip-code-but-one from Robert Dana who revived the *North American Review* in the 1960s and served later as Iowa's second poet laureate and to serve myself through most of my years knowing him as editor of a companion magazine in Iowa City.

Marilynne Robinson once said that apprentice writers don't realize they have the reader's attention and are afraid of holding it and I was thinking of that when Rebecca told me the bloodroot had returned, when I had worried after a winter of ice laid down and holding under snow that fell again and again that they lay smothered and dead now goldfinches wore their courting colors and it was a whole month later than bloodroot had appeared before, and I wondered whether they had waited for her since she had spent over a month in North Dakota and she has always been the first finder of bloodroot, which, having survived eons with no help from us, should know quite well how to survive Iowa winters. So I shouldn't have been surprised when Rebecca returned to spot those small, curled, grayish thumbs pushing up through old leaves, sticks, pine cones, dog turds, wind-tossed twigs from the evergreens, and a crow's wing our dogs had found—bloodroot had come around again to show that its author is no apprentice.

At the Linn Street Café for a pre-reading dinner, with Rebecca seated across from Clark Blaise, that evening's reader and guest of honor, he misconstrued a question of hers to ask, "What gives you the authority?" to which he replied, "Experience," but Jorie Graham jumped in with "No, the sentence," and Rebecca, once a Divinity student, heard the World from the Word, that old story.

For "In the beginning was the Word," the ground and source of everything, as an Old English Riddle (#47) makes a joke of when its bookworm chews holes in vellum leaves. The worm eats words and swallows them—word *fraet, forswealg*; who knew the expression was that old?—thus destroying, from its foundation up, some man's speech and thought. For the Word is mud that Turtle pulls from beneath deep water to form earth for men and women who then enter that myth to stand upon, as we stand our ground, upon our word, we who were but mud ourselves before breath filled us so words could spill from our tongues and lay down a path to step out on into our lives.

In his *Autobiography,* William Carlos Williams celebrated the little magazine as "one magazine, not several . . . a continuous magazine, the only one . . . with an absolute freedom of editorial policy and a succession of proprietorships that follows a democratic rule. There is absolutely no dominating policy permitting anyone to dictate anything. When it is in any way successful, it is because it fills a need in someone's mind to keep going. When it dies, someone else takes it up in some other part of the country—quite by accident—out of a desire to get the writing down on paper. . . . A person does it . . . a fallible person, subject to devotions and accidents." Moreover, he concluded, "The little magazine never more than barely kept going. . . . It is only in the aggregate that they maintained a steady trickle of excellence, mixed with the bad, that served to keep writing loose, ready to accept the early, the sensitive acquisition to art."

One afternoon Mark Strand rode his high reputation into town and the room was small and broad and modern and crowded, a modest arena, and Marvin Bell made the introduction while

Strand stood to the side, aloof I thought though perhaps just shy, wearing a pale linen sport jacket over a sand-washed tee of the lightest pink, and Jorie sat on a cement step toward the front on the left for she and Strand had arrived at the last moment and the room was full and although she had twice graced the cover of *American Poetry Review,* she was not yet of an age when a student might offer her his seat. Marvin began by recounting a time he had stayed in D.C., where Strand lived, and the two had played telephone tag since they were old mates, which, after a couple of exchanges, caused the desk clerk at his hotel, a pretty young woman, to ask whether Marvin's message had come from "Mark Strand, the Poet," to which Marvin answered, "Yes, he's handsome, isn't he," which caused the young woman to reply, "I wouldn't know; I've only read his poems," and that is when Jorie gasped, and rocked in place on the hard step, her head down, her long hair shielding her face, her knees drawn up to her chin.

Amidst the forty-five shelves in our office, some holding incoming manuscripts, some recent issues of the thirty or so magazines with whom we exchange issues, one range storing the whole history of *The Iowa Review,* two others with reference works, the *Chicago Manual of Style* (in an outdated edition), dictionaries, encyclopedias, atlases, a bible or two and other compendia of information and lore, with one whole bookcase for review copies, all interspersed by a four-drawer file cabinet and the desks of three graduate assistants, each with its computer, with another on a table along the south wall, an old metal typing table, jammed with wings folded against a door that therefore didn't open, a table that once held an IBM Selectric that I used to wheel out for envelopes before I found it easier to address those by hand, there's a coat rack behind which a fishing rod leaned in the corner, one that had belonged to my very first graduate assistant, of whom I was reminded just last week by an occasional contributor in New York, though from Nebraska in fact, who mentioned his name. Who knew they knew each other? His pole stood in that corner for over twenty years until one Sunday I tossed it in the dumpster.

All this in one twelve by twenty foot room with a conference table in its center, a southeast window looking out over a parking lot and railroad tracks beyond which one can see the library, six or eight chairs we're always shoving aside or stumbling over, and several house plants, with broad, green leaves on long, drooping stems that Lynne, our Managing Editor, has added, and waters, you could find—"David's Shelf"—one shelf for letters and manuscripts that I wouldn't leave to others no matter how veteran, work that came, usually, from former contributors to whom I felt some relation, or from a school kid or farm wife, a penitentiary inmate, or a university colleague who doesn't read contemporary writing but may have written some of it, or a writer from a distant culture, unschooled in SASEs, who has no idea of our magazine and what it attempts and that for some reason I hoped to answer rather than dump. All these possible treasures waited on my shelf for my attention, which I always intended. Every day I intended to answer more as I proved the bottleneck of our provident order, a neck I narrow further for ruminations like these that form another shelf, you could say, for some purpose that is far from clear.

Magazines as storerooms of ammunition, reviews re-view, while "journal" derives from Jupiter, whose shining, diurnal face scans the world each day, reading over our shoulders.

From the very beginning, the challenge that interested me most was the choices we made, for what's the point of a magazine if it does not print good stuff, and the best way of finding that is by reading a lot, unsolicited offerings for the most part, often by writers with little or no publishing record though the writer may make claims in a cover letter and usually does, to which we pay as little attention as possible. Not that we mind the letter itself for it is a courtesy to acknowledge this odd human relationship of writer to reader and back. But we generally find whatever claims made beside the point once into the work, from which we emerge, far more often than not, uncertain for want of a controlling theory of value to which we had committed ourselves and that we try to avoid in hopes of being fair minded readers which, if it means anything, may mean readers at a fair and minded, that is supplied with something like a mind, by that fact.

Of course "To Autumn" is a marvelous poem. Generations of teachers have told us so and thousands of hours of class time have gone into inventing reasons why, but what of "To February" by Susan Wilberforce whose name I've contrived though she no doubt exists and if I've anticipated a poem of hers, she should send it to us but with SASE since I have often wondered what we would have done with a small packet from Emily D had she sent half a dozen poems in the conventional manner before her name was known beyond Amherst.

I thought I would meet myself face to face, over my tastes and values, that over time my choices would become my definition and I that much better known to myself. For magazines ride on the judgment of their editors, which they expose for their readers, even unto embarrassment, and so as I became better known to myself, the work should have become easier which was the surprise, that I never stopped laboring over making those choices and found it rare to read and know an absolute, unqualified "Yes" and put down far too many manuscripts thinking I'd come back to them later for I must have missed something though I approached all that finally with a certain despair since, perhaps, the reader I met over all those years just wasn't the one I set out to discover.

Jane Kenyon's "American Triptych" came unsolicited my first year, a three-part poem that anchored her first book, and I warmed to "the repeated clink of a flagpole / pulley in the driveway of a country store," or "chilled" you could say since it reran that shiver up my spine of standing out on the playground in winter, in a coat not warm enough, near a flagless pole, waiting for the bell to ring so we could race inside, the clink of the chain on the pole like ice in my blood.

According to an article in the *Times*, "an overwhelming majority of Chicago's public school students—some 85 percent, according to federal statistics—live in poverty," and "32 school-age children were killed" last year, with 24 more murdered so far this; and though I believe with Williams that men (and women) die every day for wont of what can be found in poems, I am still at a loss before such facts.

A year after her death, Gerald Stern mentioned that he and Phil Levine had spent the afternoon before sitting on his front porch reading Jane's poems aloud to each other and reciting passages they had by heart.

The annoying buzz finally got to Michael Cunningham, who grew up in Los Angeles and looked up from his desk one afternoon to wink at a friend who was also from L.A. and declare, gently but firmly, "San Francisco's for losers," perhaps even then planning his move to New York where he could keep up with another on our staff, a young woman we both feared anorexic, and for the sake of, and with whom, Michael plotted escapes for milkshakes at the Memorial Union. Coming back from one such outing, having carried manuscripts along, he reentered calling out, "Hey, you've got to read this," this being "Alfred Kinsey, Alone After an Interview, Dreams of Indiana," which became one of Michael Martone's first published stories.

My informal seminar, with nothing to grade, in which many have instructive moments, as well as moments of being my instructor.

Walking Ramón along the Iowa River, I passed a fisherman who offered me his catch. I was outward bound on a warm September afternoon, had no need for them either, and though I had a plastic bag I was carrying it for another purpose, so I declined, but the fisherman persisted, a second time and a third until I relented and he filled my sack with two hefty catfish, not entirely dead. Taking my fish-laden sack in one hand and the leash in the other, I continued with Ramón and that's when he met Donald Justice, as Ramón should have done, "Pale Ramón" being his secret name and Wallace Stevens one of Don's poets. Don was off in the distance, walking toward us, high stepping, almost marching under the late summer sun and making, I first thought, the sign of the cross, repeatedly, up, down, left, right, his eyes fixed on the walk so intently that he was startled, and slightly embarrassed to be caught out as we came abreast of each other. "Oh, hello, I was composing something," which by then I had guessed as he paused to pat Ramón and spoke of being fond of dogs. Ramón, a nervous mutt from a shelter, always ready to bolt from strange men, especially when bearded, on a bike, and in shorts as Don was not, stood patiently under Don's touch. Then we turned and fell in together, two men, one dog, a dark Collie-mix with the tan brows of a shepherd, and two catfish flopping in a plastic sack, which we all tried to ignore as we spoke of the new school year, of a conference on Frost from which I had just returned—"For years my favorite," Don had said on another occasion—of the river beside us and its own rising and falling over the summer. While the fish squirmed more and more, one slipping almost out of the sack until by the time we had strolled another couple of hundred yards they made conversation all but impossible. But by then we were upon a construction site where several cement blocks lay about. It's strange how determined to hold onto something one can become. I could have dumped the fish in the river and suffered no loss but felt I had earned them and had dinner in mind when Don, anticipating my solution, offered to take Ramón off my hands, which he did, one gentleman leading another to the riverbank where they stood with their backs to me, watching the water flow quietly past, while I battered the heads of two slippery catfish against a cement block.

"Don't be afraid to get a firm grasp on the obvious," my old professor had advised.

There are many reasons for a literary review, but one I have always felt counted most. Everything else is peripheral to our saying "Yes" to writers we do not know, writers who didn't emerge from our circle, who may have sent their work from anywhere and who have found favor so far only where they were assented to by friends, which is a fine way to start, so natural that it is hard to imagine another, but to submit that same work to strangers and hear them say, "Hey, you are coming through to us"—that I always thought was our best reason for being.

A mature white pine stands outside my study window, so close that branches reach our eaves, and I've hung a feeder filled with sunflower seed about fifteen feet away and right in view as the small birds come and I relish the titmice, the rarest of the regulars, who fly in one at a time, take a seed and bring it to a smaller branch, little more than a twig but nearer my window and framed by it as if to present themselves, "Here I am, Titmouse, hammering away at your seed" though maybe he doesn't say "Titmouse" but like the Fox, who are the Meskwaki, prefers his own name. Perhaps the "peet" or "keet" that I hear them pipe, stating their name, or calling mine, or their mate, or perhaps for more seed—"seet, seet, seet"—the repetitions varying from one to five that I count as I count on their return to our feeder.

I found myself reading and setting some work aside for maybe I'd see more in it a second time, then setting it aside again, still unwilling to reject it, when what I should have learned is that hesitation means "No," although there were a few times, very few, when a second or fourth reading brought out something persuasive that I'd not noticed before, which helped me remember that an instant decision suggested I knew ahead of time what I was looking for when I preferred to believe that I waited to be surprised.

Sitting around our table, whatever group of us that year, we read poems aloud to each other, poems by strangers, and found, in an early instance,

> I took the old man in me
> & went to the river.
> Get out, I said
> opening my coat
> to tree & air & ice.
> Get out, I said. This is it.

Which was enough for us to take "Passage" and two more poems by Marianne Boruch, then studying in Taiwan, and who came back to us every few years thereafter.

And a few lines about a white hart,

> Some who followed what was presumed to be his trail
> Found the purple knobflax said to grow only
> From his hoof marks, and some became engulfed
> By celina moths thought to spring from his urine,

107

foreshadowing her erotic evocations of nature, always an amalgam of the imagined and the exact, led us to "The Success of the Hunt," our first poem by Pattiann Rogers, who said years later that it was important to her because her style was changing and the change was not welcome to earlier readers, but our acceptance helped her accept it in herself.

There is the way of being tribal and asserting over and over the primacy of your tribe while maneuvering to amass more audience for it, and even though I'm sure that appears our way to some, and has its own reasons for being, it was never the way I favored.

Like Williams, I like to think of literary magazines as a single magazine, a jerry-rigged patchwork of many small readerships adding up to one large alternative magazine, springing up here, there, and all over, a dandelion patch of a magazine with seeds drifting far and wide, an ironic franchise with numerous local providers, each issue something like a bagel, in flavors that vary, and with, very likely, a hole in its middle—but not junk food and possibly scrumptious.

In the case of Dionisio D. Martínez, I can't remember now whether it was,

> My father sold firewood
> across the river when he was ten.
> He walked by his horse, running
> his hands up and down the reins
> and thinking of his mother,
> how she stayed home, running
> her hands up and down the rosary . . .

or,

> You have a hunger for the Latin boys, always
>   standing at the edge
> of a trend. You softshoe your way into the heart of

> anyone with
> a pair of dark eyes and a good radio. . . .

I pick up Alfred Kazin's *A Walker in the City,* a book I should have read years ago but find in a new paper edition at Prairie Lights and pause on its first page at the "instant rage" that comes over Kazin when he returns to his Brownsville neighborhood, and I think of how often "rage" and "bitterness" come into Stern's poems. "Bitter" must be one of his key words although in person he tends toward the buoyant. He even came to faculty meetings no other writer bothered to attend. Maybe that was the old union organizer in him. But reasons for bitterness are there that I cannot share without pretense, and I realize it has taken most of my life to find, through him, the Psalms and Lamentations essential to our lyric tradition.

Yusef Komunyakaa came to us first through the slush in the very early 90s with a poem called "Work" in which a young black man mowing a lawn on a hot summer day negotiates his physical distance from and feigns indifference to an underdressed young white woman sunbathing beside the family pool even though she is not entirely averse to making eye contact. The poem recalled a graduate school summer I spent working for a small business installing pools and building fences, the crew made up of young black men from the neighborhood, except for me, the white guy. I had the special assignment of service visits to pools already installed. A couple of mornings each week I made my rounds of Albemarle County, alone in a pickup, precisely so the African Americans on our crew would not compromise, or be compromised by, a scantily clothed white woman. Then I returned to afternoons of fence construction with the other guys, who accepted me into their rail-stringing and posthole-digging with more grace than I had earned, though I tried.

At the very end of the *Divine Comedy,* Dante imagines Divine Presence as three colorful circles of equal dimension, one reflected by another as rainbow by rainbow while the third seems fire breathed forth by the other two, a trinity that captivates the seeker wholly as he stands in peace within the divine arena of the celestial white rose. I have tried to understand those three circles as mirrors that reflect all of creation from all points of view and so wholly absorb one's spirit and sight. And some late afternoons, knocking down Dante's gorgeous thought just a peg or two more, I have seen them as three spheres, the elements of a little magazine, writers, readers, and staff, each necessary and in some unfathomable way a product of the other two, and which, as an imagined perfection, are all one needs of this world.

II

Chickadee flies onto the feeder but Nuthatch is there to fend him off, so Chickadee pops up to a limb on the little hackberry beside it, taking his perch, awaiting his turn, and Nuthatch seems pleased to keep him waiting so after a few moments Chickadee turns to grooming, lifting one wing then the other to peck away beneath it.

"Scrape," "scratch," "scrawl," and "scribe" all come from the same Indo-European root, which leads as well to "engrave" and "gravid," the manual labor of writing having always got smoother until words coast upon light on a screen and become lighter words, always less lapidary, by stages. That the change should correlate with our beginning to shun writing's old male chauvinist aura complicates but does not alter the underlying condition, for I doubt that we have advanced as technicians of the craft because of a feminist desire to disable writing's long association with the impregnation of the word by the almighty pen. So far men have accomplished most of the technological monkeying around, and though I can fancy we did it as self-castration, ridding ourselves of our most troublesome instrument, like crazed Attis in that poem by Catullus, I am not persuaded.

I'm old enough to have practiced ways that are quaint, carbon copies for example, and when I began my dissertation, I treated myself to a Smith-Corona, portable, electric typewriter, the state of the art then though it still lacked a correcting ribbon; and I was charmed to find the same typewriter in Marianne Moore's Greenwich Village room as reconstructed by the Rosenbach Museum in Philadelphia where it stands beside her small wooden desk from *The Dial,* which, for several years, she edited. To have overlapped with her practice bemused me though I liked even more the thought of her carrying a padded folding chair out through the window and onto a rooftop of her apartment building where she is said to have written poems, inscribing in longhand her first drafts.

A colleague observes that readers go to theory today for what they used to get from Hemingway, Fitzgerald, Faulkner, and others, but neither Jacques Derrida nor Fredric Jameson has drawn crowds like John Ashbery, in his dark blue shirt, tan sport coat, and flowered tie, his thinning hair neatly combed, his voice expressionless but for traces of deadpan humor as he mentioned a detail that had prompted one poem or another when a man who had interrupted on other occasions spoke up from the far side of the auditorium, with threat in his voice and without making clear what he expected. Ashbery didn't panic but listened, reclaimed the floor, and after a third uncalled for remark altered his order to read a different poem, "Yes, Dr. Grenzmer, How May I Be of Assistance to You? What! Do You Say the Patient Has Escaped?" Laughter swept the room and the "patient," bless him, waited it out, shouted "Bravo!" and settled back in his seat for the remainder of the reading.

An editor encourages writers by observing that the numbers they face, our heaps of unsolicited manuscripts, aren't all that overwhelming since so little competes for our best attention, which suggests that old notion of being able to tell at a glance, in a paragraph, by the first page or two, whether you've found art, something I am almost never able to manage.

With first the electric typewriter and then the computer, writers spoke earnestly of the quicker way as suspicious and permissible only for writing unworthy of our deeper feelings and thoughts. One might write business letters that way, or committee reports, or letters of recommendation, but stories and poems still required digging in with pen (or pencil) on paper. Someone must have thought similarly of the fountain pen as opposed to the quill, and later of that gentle felt tip.

Overheard in the mall, "Of course I know Donald Justice, I like Donald Justice, but it's not as if I'm going to become Donald Justice."

According to Mary Oppen, Louis Zukofsky, the poet, was annoyed with her husband, George, also a poet, for not preferring Zukofsky's poetry to his own. But Oppen shrugged off Zukofsky's dismay: why should he not prefer his own poems, "They're mine, aren't they?" One wonders whether Zukofsky always took care to prefer Ezra Pound and William Carlos Williams.

Proofreading expresses our Faith in the Dream of Perfection, the pride we take in approaching that, but now and then mistakes have their moment, such as the line that I wished least to correct: "Loose bottoms on her blouse were seldom preludes to seduction."

The increasing ease of the manual labor of writing quickly found its way to submissions, which were once singular, only an original typescript would do, leading a writer, often, to refold his rejected poems and stories and send them right out again, and again, until their multiple handlings betrayed too much. Simultaneous submissions followed from and were made conceivable by Xerox and the office printer. When carbon made the copy, an original meant something. Dot matrix printers made weakly printed texts, often very hard to read. Suddenly a Xerox proved more legible, so it could be construed as more courteous to send a copy. Within a short time, laser printers became the norm. Now the original text has no meaning, there being no indentation on the page, no digging in of type, and one can't tell the original from a copy unless signed with blue ink.

It was Auden who observed that cuisine was, of all the arts, the most widespread at the highest level of accomplishment. But that was before MFA programs.

The first time we received a laser printed text as a submission, I assumed, from its professional look, especially the series of line drawings illustrating the Western Roll and Fosbury Flop, that it was an off-print sent for my amusement and tossed it on my shelf for an idle moment. It took a couple of months for me to catch up with advancing practice and say, "Whoa, that was a submission," then look, laugh, and accept Mark Axelrod's "Metaleptic Parabasis *or* The Fine Art of High Jumping," a tongue-in-cheek disquisition on the language of criticism, followed a few years later by his account of the Russian origins of baseball.

Perhaps we could propose a feminist slant to all this and venture that the loss of a meaningful original is analogous to undermining primogeniture, that old identification of a unique and uniquely legitimate male heir. Now as more generous mothers of our work, we propagate widely, with equal affection for all our offspring, if you'll buy that.

A summer night and a bat in our house, and knowing of guys whacking at it with a tennis racket or stumbling around hoping to trap it in a towel, I stumbled on a solution: turn all the lights on upstairs, then in the back rooms downstairs, and open the front door.

Williams Carlos Williams again, "The first thing to do in hearing poems is not to try to understand them at the start at least…. Let the poem come to you," phrasing that has moved on to basketball.

The late Jim Simmerman was the only submitter from whom I welcomed multi-page cover letters, full of play and a few pointers about reading his poems, a rhyme to look for, "the only one for 'orange'" in one case though that proved a stretch. Once he sent a four-page poem in ballad-like quatrains in the midst of which comes a scene of sister-brother fellatio. Can I include this, I asked myself and then thought, why not; anyone who has read this far will be in sympathy. Few will even see it; let it be a test. A woman in Davenport had once written, "You are denounced," objecting to sex in "Home," a Jayne Anne Phillips story still alive and well in her collection, *Black Tickets*. So we included Jim's poem, to echoing silence, until a letter came from Boston, hand written, ball point pen on yellow legal paper, commending us on our daring treatment of a delicate and neglected subject and hoping the writer could count on more of that nature, to which I said nothing. What could I say, how could I promise? So her letter went in a file of curiosities and we went on only to receive a second letter a couple of weeks later, this time from Buffalo, handwritten again though not clearly by the same person yet making the same request and suggesting that our touching on the forbidden was balm to her wounded life, and I added that to the file, wondering about the new minority we and our grave digger—"Digger" being the name of the poem—had unearthed, the odd chance that we were looked to by it, and wondering if the letters might be a joke, but afraid also of hurting a writer's feelings by presuming as much. So things stood until the following summer when I visited my sister-in-law who kept goats outside Philadelphia and made cheese for restaurants, and as I stood in her shed watching her milk, she asked, "Have you got any strange mail recently," and the charade was up. She had, however, passed the test.

For an all-poetry issue, I wanted to represent American poetries widely and corralled two guest co-editors, one a student of the Language Poets and the avant-garde, the other an African Native American woman whose parallel area, an equally challenging avant-garde in my view, is work born of Otherness. I in turn would solicit a sampling of past contributors and add some of what came regularly through the mail, our wrinkle being that we would lay out our contents alphabetically rather than segregate them by tribes so edges would blur and one might not always know who was who and what what. See Zaarcluz, for example, at the end of that issue. So one afternoon I outlined my plan to Don Justice and let him know that his work would be welcome but, as I suspected, he wasn't keen on my idea and said he thought not. Within weeks though his *New and Selected Poems* came out, featuring a painting of his on its dust jacket. I wrote quickly—"Where there is work like this there must be more"—and suggested a year of his art on our covers. Thus a long, narrow painting of a railroad yard in Florida welcomes readers to the issue of which he declined to be part.

"Be moderate, be decent, be brief," a writer from Spain quotes me, with apparent approval, as having said, and I receive his letter on the very day I accept Curtis White's story, "Maverick," in large part because it is immoderate, indecent, and a little on the longish side.

Our office as an island, with a mail drop view of the world, and I've long been attracted to islands, not just the willow strewn sandbars of the Missouri in whose floodplain we farmed but, because of a winter travelogue series at our local library when I was about ten, Hawaii and New Zealand, lush flora and fauna, especially the birds, and long, sweeping beaches, and by now I've visited Mackinac, Ossabaw, Oahu, Kauai, Madeira, Mallorca, and Great Britain, on which my total residence has been, perhaps, six months, but enough for me to imagine looking out over surf as I stand at the window and toss message-bearing bottles on waves breaking over the parking lot.

I ask my graduate assistants about a reading the night before, poets on tour for a Best Young Poets anthology, and one answers that it was okay but she guessed she preferred "our own aesthetic," to which others nod, which is to say familiarity plays a large part in recognizing something we like, which is to say that had our poets read in Ann Arbor, Charlottesville, or Santa Cruz they too could have been shrugged off as audiences favored their home team, which is to say something remarkable happens, x-part quality and y-part hype, with hype the smaller part we hope, when a poet transcends that home field advantage and becomes widely read and heard. And which helps explain why the Best Young Poets of only a few years ago, even poets who emerged from here, can be read with indifference by our

Best Young Poets Today since yesterday's poets have gone off and taken their familiarity with them.

What to make of that peculiar American institution of running our literature all but entirely through the universities as if by now they were the only ground for art; as if Gertrude Stein, Robert Frost, Marianne Moore, Langston Hughes, Ezra Pound, Elizabeth Bishop, Ernest Hemingway, William Faulkner, Zora Neale Hurston, W. E. B. DuBois, Henry David Thoreau, and many more should now be at the mercy of MFA programs for permission to publish; as if, without a faculty position in an MFA program one has little claim on being a writer; as if our workshops had not become programs in rhetoric as much as in poetics, the rhetoric of students vying for the acclaim of each other, and of their instructors, who in turn depend upon the approval of those students; as if seasonal tastes for what's cool, cultivated in hothouse workshops, were not a notion with a bit of wilt on it.

For years I resisted the annual Convention of Associated Writing Programs, wondering why I should want to meet hundreds of writers whom I had rejected. But I could not resist a trip to Palm Springs and found it was fun. "Like a high school reunion without the jocks" (that's Michael Martone), and I laughed even though in high school jockdom had been my ambition. Not that I was any good at it. But writers came by our table, pleased with how they had appeared in our pages. Some valued comments in letters and notes from me or from one of our staff; others wished to speak of writing we found that they particularly valued—"Remember that story by Robert Boswell? It meant a lot to me." Or at a coffee shop with a writer I have favored, I reminisce about his work and that of his Fiction Collective 2 confederates, all the while avoiding mention of another story we ran, long ago, one of my all time favorites, because, just possibly, his use, some might say his ripping off of it, could become a delicate subject. But writing has permeable boundaries and is written to be appropriated and made something else of.

In *The Pound Era*, Hugh Kenner reports Pound confessed that although he had arranged for Joyce's publication in *The Little Review*, he himself didn't understand Joyce at all and had not managed to finish *Ulysses*, but he knew, from having met him, that Joyce "had it."

Rob Stilwell wore the attitude of the poet perfectly and seemed, often, The Poet among us, especially when off on a ramble linking Mozart, Wordsworth, and Bob Dylan. When I looked him up years later, living with his mother, he had just mowed the lawn and spent the last hour on his knees, hand clipping grass under a chainlink fence. He led my daughter and me on a tour of his hometown, Columbus, Indiana, identifying architects for Jenny, an interest of hers, and commenting learnedly on them as we paused at the public library designed by I. M. Pei so he could return a few books and check out another armload then drove past other public buildings by Gunnar Birkerts and Eliel Saarinen. Later he took us down into the basement where his collection of LPs and manuscripts, gathered in cardboard boxes, were arranged around the room as if each were a seat at a roundtable of worthies—but without the table. The number of manuscripts had easily doubled since I had last seen him, including over 1100 poems of 11 lines each, dictated by an aesthetic quite private, and he pored over his folders, looking for work to show me but settled on reading us a few poems. So we had a private reading, Jenny and I, seated in semi-lotus positions on his basement, indoor-outdoor carpeting.

Pound knew Joyce, Williams, H.D., and Eliot. James Laughlin sought Pound out and through him came to know the others, around whom he built New Directions, for the stranger the work is, the more likely it will ride first on the ethos of the writer. So it was with Black Mountain, the Harlem Renaissance, and so more recently with the Language poets. In contrast, the university review, which maintains and celebrates the virtues of inacquaintance, is circumscribed by what its editor has already come to know, which, rather more than less, I take to be close to natural law.

As I learned from Donald Hall, who revised Michael Roberts' influential *Faber Book of Modern Verse* (1936). Roberts had left out Frost and Thomas Hardy on the grounds that their omission enabled him to define the modern. Respecting Roberts' intentions in his revision three decades later, Hall too left Frost and Hardy out though he added Williams, whom Roberts had not had the chance to know. Then he added Richard Wilbur and Philip Larkin, Hall's limits of the modern being wider than Roberts', but not all-inclusive as they did not encompass Robert Creeley, who failed to be one of the thirty-five poets Hall added, among whom we find Theodore Roethke, John Berryman, Robert Lowell, and Wilbur—but not Robert Hayden or Elizabeth Bishop; Robert Bly, Louis Simpson, W. D. Snodgrass, W. S. Merwin, James Wright, and Sylvia Plath—but not Ashbery, Creeley, Justice, Stern, or Levine. Hall also confessed once that he had turned down Frank O'Hara and Allen Ginsberg, "Howl" in fact, for *The Paris Review*. How hard it is to read what we have not already assimilated and understood.

"Let me take a bunch with me," I pleaded with Rob; "I'll put some in our magazine." "No, no," he wasn't ready but maybe he'd send me something in a week or two, or he would meet me in Louisville three weeks later and bring poems with him then. But he didn't come to Louisville, which would have been a short drive, nor did he answer his phone, and now another quarter century has passed.

Could Rob be a Dickinson of our day, failed by his Thomas Higginson, me? Should I have stolen those boxes and prepared his "Collected" before a first volume had come out? Here is one of the 1100:

With the Key of Softness

> writing to each other
>   despite these many distances
> we shall grasp back no bodies out of Death
>   but at least can all ways feel
> rather like two cold winged and minor Angels
>   poised with enamel azure for some antique
> apocryphal yet aureate figured Gospels Book
>   in viewless union sent to bear off one
> gray pitted wedge of even this heaviest coral
>   shattered across our thousand year old grave
> white roses there or sea shells carved from light

Rob is my epitome, my classic special case, but there have been many and each year brings a new sampling. A writer from Dubuque who signed only with initials and sent poems my first year when I was least prepared to deal with them and who I still think of as possibly singular; the ex-CEO from Des Moines who turned to poetry again in retirement; Ruth Doty who had written with her husband as M. R. Doty until Mark assented to his sexuality while she stayed in Des Moines and wrote notes to me from time to time, with apologies for taking my time, some of which I answered before she died, much too soon. The ex-Workshopper, unheard from in thirty years, who had played horse with Strand and made notebooks of her poems and sent several. I don't publish books, I apologized, sliding away. The retired doctor who begins his memoirs by narrating an emergency housecall by sleigh through a snowstorm at night in Newfoundland. The gentleman from Cedar Rapids who complained that I couldn't possibly have seen a better sonnet all year, not by an Iowan. A former neighbor, a law professor who came out, left his family, moved to Vermont and started writing stories and published a novel. Someone met on a plane; a prisoner; several prisoners; former students; another retired law professor who offered haiku; each one seeking affiliation that just might begin with me; each one capable—why should I presume otherwise?—of providing the manuscript that I alone would see as special and grab onto and offer happily as "an early, a sensitive acquisition to art."

At the lunch counter to which we had driven almost as soon as I arrived at their door, Jane Kenyon sat on Hall's left and I on his right attempting conversation while Jane stared straight ahead over her grilled cheese sandwich, and I forced the extra time required to toast bread for a BLT. White bread, with coffee of the sort we rarely drink anymore, and I caught on gradually to Jane's strained, almost monosyllabic attempts at civility as sufficient sign of her depression's being in charge and that I should beat a retreat as soon as we got back to Eagle Pond, their farm. Don and I could return to writing letters.

The indigo buntings affirm their commitment to our yard and I go to Ace Hardware for seed to affirm my end of the bargain, and Oriole too has returned though I have yet to find him high in the cottonwood just leafing out but I recognize his song, not the series of round piping tones I first learned but single notes as if testing and studying to sing until a Cooper's hawk crosses the ravine to the broken maple beside the patio where he perches, watching me on our deck not twenty feet away, and eyeing the birdbath, then me again while stepping closer and more into the open before he floats down to the bath's rim and walks all around it, looking for the best spot to drink, and over his shoulder constantly—who could his predator be, in daylight when the owl sleeps—and he dips his head, sips twice and flies off to the fence on the north side of our yard. Then across the ravine and away while Oriole, way up high in that cottonwood, keeps quiet.

I had visited one earlier, sunnier weekend and had walked up into old pastures with them and with Gus, their dog, and around the pond, hearing Jane call Don "Perkins" while Don pointed out Mt. Kearsarge and we made time for an interview broken up by drop-ins of old friends, Richard Eberhart and Daniel Ellsberg to name two—who didn't he know?—with Creeley, if I remember correctly, due to arrive a day or so later. They'd barely have time to change the sheets. This had all been prompted by the chance, as I began, of my finding it helpful to talk to someone not from here and so writing him a letter excused, I hoped, by their having written a kind note to me after stumbling upon a poem of mine. But I had no idea of his enthusiasm for correspondence, or that I would keep up with him until email led me astray. And it took years to learn how he taped his part for a typist in the neighborhood to turn, as we now say, to hard copy, nor of the number of writers he corresponded with, like a chess master moving from table to table, with gusto, which of course encouraged mine. All our musing about poetry and favorite writers. Hardy's image, "she who in the dark world shows / As a lattice-gleam when midnight moans." He and Jane read to each other in the evening and at one point were working through the "Prefaces" of Henry James. And our gossip, with a little chiding now and then as when I failed to take poems sent by a girlfriend, possibly, of a pal of his, to which I was able to reply, "Oh come on" and he to admit his having failed to take "Howl," all of which brought us to the pond and pasture, to tie-ups in the barn and the old maple from which his grandfather had hung, for him, a swing.

I drove up once more, late winter and gray, and he took me to Jane's grave. Leaves of the autumn before lay strewn around and mementos were laid out on her headstone, sea shells, a poem torn from a paper and left under pebbles, a locket, a ballpoint pen, and we stopped to buy a *Boston Globe* at the country store where a chain clinked in the cold against a metal flagpole.

"He doesn't hold back, does he?" Rebecca observed when I read aloud Hall's "Letter with No Address" in which he finds Jane's Saab, its trunk lid "delicately raised, / as if proposing an encounter" with his Honda, and "Conversation's Afterplay"— "'Shh, shh,' you said. / 'I want to put my legs around your head'"—and "Tennis Ball" in which Hall, walking Gus in the cemetery where Jane lies, notices that Gus notices four long naked legs unshielded by a gravestone and distracts him from investigating further but can't resist a backward glance as he and Gus return to the car. The next morning, Rebecca woke up asking, "Did he really say she 'restarted' him?"

III

Stavros Deligiorgis gave me a copy of *Muriel Foster's Fishing Diary*, an out-of-print book that a fly fisherwoman in Scotland began at Little Loch Broom in 1913 and continued for over thirty years, filling it with hundreds of watercolor sketches of fish, lures, birds and also Old Bob, her canine companion on many a trip; and I thought of using his image on our rejection slip with "Old Bob says 'Sorry'" our only remark, but when I wrote seeking permission, I was told "Sorry" for the book was coming back into print though I did pirate Old Bob for a T-shirt for our brautroast that summer and added the legend, "28 years of work to chew on."

A few days after her homecoming from six restorative weeks in North Dakota and after several days of an infection strong enough to require one long evening at the ER, with something given intravenously and antibiotics, Rebecca and I went out to our favorite bistro for pot roast, though it wasn't called pot roast but "wine-braised beef," and a bottle of Argentine red, and as we lingered, talking more and more closely, Rebecca teared-up at the thought of spring's cruel "mixing" of "memory and desire" as we had seen ourselves that afternoon noting first signs of bloodroot and bluebells, and I thought of how often, more often every year, I've noticed that every poet's theme seems to be just that, how they keep on saying it, all of them, and how I've longed to invert the cliché and imagine, with Robert Francis, becoming "friskier" instead. But the old theme is not to resist. Not unless disaster sweeps me from my perch before I have a chance to accept its forcing itself upon us like the desire we spoke of all the way home, of bluebells that spread and insist, pushing their tough, bunched leaves up between patio stones and rising again, still bloody from below, as purple as they are green, into the season they ring in for us.

"I'm having the best time in the company of my narrator," Marilynne mentioned to Rebecca one morning the summer before she published her Pulitzer Prize winning *Gilead,* as they met on a neighborhood corner, both walking dogs.

In the very first issue of *Black Mountain Review* (1954), Martin Seymour-Smith attacked Theodore Roethke's *The Waking,* which had just won the Pulitzer Prize. "Neat," Seymour-Smith called it, three times, and "dead" in its thinking. "No amount of metrical jellying along can turn what was first a prose idea into a poem," he observed before turning on Dylan Thomas. These attempted assassinations caused Kenneth Rexroth to resign from the *Review*'s board of Contributing Editors as Robert

Creeley, twenty-eight at the time, announced two issues later while remaining entirely unrepentant. Roethke's "completely adolescent address to the world" and Thomas' unchallenged authority as "major" were exactly the sort of thing that he had set himself against, and he added a definition of what he had hoped for in a Contributing Editor: "One counted on as a regular source of material—also sympathy, interest, a kind of cohort" as he described a coterie magazine that, by definition, is much surer of what it wants and less likely to be surprised. One that insists its featured writers, pals for the most part, and perhaps for that reason, are themselves that "early, sensitive acquisition to art" rather than waiting to be recognized by strangers as such.

The conundrum must be ancient: a poet cannot be a poet if she alone shouts she is but will never be a poet without believing, and saying aloud, exactly that.

"We who please ourselves with the fancy that we are the only poets, and everyone else is *prose*," Emily D wrote to Susan Gilbert, soon her sister-in-law, in an early letter.

Writing a little more than a decade after he ended *Black Mountain Review*, Creeley summarized the "rule book" for a magazine that he had received "with quick generosity and clarity" from Pound who had suggested "I get at least four others, on whom I could depend unequivocally for material, and to make their work the mainstay of the magazine's form." But then, he added, "let the rest of it, roughly half, be as various and hogwild as possible, so that any idiot thinks he has a chance of getting in."

I wanted our magazine to be distinctive, but rather than writing a credo, I assumed difference would show of its own accord. My habits of attention are hardly those of anyone else, so over time, without declaring a program, distinction should emerge. The hardest act would be making choices and that was the only act that really mattered. But we had much to choose from and our sheer dearth of pages would force me to return almost everything. If I held to work I admired, I couldn't go far wrong. No reader would have more than a glancing awareness of the rest, just as no one need know what her, or his, beloved passed over before buying that birthday present.

This morning it's Titmouse first at the sunflower seed feeder and he brings a single seed to the limb above and pecks away while sun glistens on the limb, making its upper surface shine, and on the long pine needles moving in the breeze like so many silver pompoms under bright lights. His small crest rises too, tossing in the wind, and shines like light itself, upstaging the shadow of death under which we know he, like all small creatures, constantly lives. His crest must be thinner than I had imagined, a tiny war bonnet, and his tail feathers, spread to help him keep balance, are outlined in light though he has flown off in the time it has taken me to write these few sentences and a nuthatch has come and gone in his place which is held, for the moment, by a cardinal.

Coterie magazines and university reviews: Williams wrote of the former to which the greater part of magazine romance accrues, which stems from their bravado, a quick, unquiet force that may soon subside. *Blast* put out but two issues, *The Black Mountain Review* five, and four (one a double issue) were enough for *Locus Solus* by John Ashbery and friends, whereas I came to see the university review as like the Agricultural Extension Services of land-grant universities, reasonably secure with modest institutional backing and willing to entertain submissions from citizens near and far, far enough off in most cases to cross our threshold as strangers.

One lively vessel among little magazines was Cid Corman's *Origin*, coming out in five series from Massachusetts to Japan from the early 50s through the mid 80s, with intervals of calm as Corman discovered new sources of camaraderie and inspiration. "A quarterly for the creative," he called it, copies of which could be had "for love" but "not for money." He only printed 300 at a time and invited readers to write and request them. Libraries were to approach him as any other reader: "I deal only with minorities of one," he advised.

kayak, George Hitchcock's devotion, "not a galleon, ark, coracle, or speedboat" and always with the small "k," bobbed up for over fifty issues and is remembered for its witty rejection slips, visual as far as I ever knew, taken from western dime novels: a cowpoke shot off his mount, or pitched to the street through a saloon's swinging doors, or swung from his horse by a rope.

Another, for a few issues, very few I suspect, I only saw one and it was Number Two, was *Assemblings*, put out by Richard Kostelanetz, who invited contributions from writers to whom he felt connected who obliged him with a thousand copies each of whatever they had made, which he assembled into so many copies of an issue.

Kostelanetz sent his own work far and wide and some came our way, a few pieces of which struck me as just right and went into our magazine, and I was always amused by his solution to that nuisance of the SASE; rather than sending a stamped return envelope, he sent checks for 39 or 72 cents, whatever it had cost to send us his work, shrewd in his guess that we'd never bother to take that to a bank but would put our own stamps on returns to him. Which sometimes we did and sometimes neglected so that his work could get stuck on "David's Shelf" until ditched.

One piece of his, experimental, perhaps, audacious, sexy, more than a touch pornographic, consisted of one hundred twenty-eight sex stories in a graduating then diminishing series, the first story one word long, the second two, all the way to sixty-four words, that twice, then descending to one again, the words arranged in columns across the page, seven columns as soon as a story came to that length, somewhat

as	if	each	word	were	an	erogenous
zone	just	waiting	to	be	brushed	lightly
by	a	reader's	naked	eye	and	so

quicken like flesh. Some of those quick takes got quite hot and I thought it a lot of fun and accepted the story, or stories, only to decide on a kill-fee later and return the whole with a small check once I imagined and then felt guilty about my graduate assistants, a young man and a young woman, having to proofread those stories aloud to each other and mouth all those moments of inserting this or that into that or this. My protectiveness quaint even then, several years already after a woman first said "fuck" aloud in one of my classes, perhaps not only to prove that she too could. But I returned the story, with my apologetic check, using our postage, though not really in all that much doubt as to whether I had suppressed an early, sensitive, acquisition to art.

Why does experimental fiction turn so often to sex? If experiment is the point, wouldn't writing about a closet full of shoes prove the greater challenge? But it does hold our attention, as Robert Coover said somewhere or other.

And I was censoring a writer, one whose experiment had much to do with transgression, when the whole idea of a literary magazine may be that transgression is what counts, though one must also admit that all choices enact a degree of censorship, one thing selected while we let go of a few dozen or several hundred others, each for subjective reasons, a censorship of taste, or of program, or of knowing beforehand, at least more or less, what belongs between our covers.

"Have you reformed yet?" the senator inquired at a statehouse luncheon. "Have you accepted yet the first amendment?" I replied as we approached each other. He had been a gentleman, calling first to inform me of his objection to an issue and his plan to challenge state support of the university because of it. Our administration in turn told me to "relax," although they very likely grimaced, as one might to some stories under the rubric, "Transgressions." One can sympathize with parents objecting to the discovery in a high school library of a story in which a feverish girl masturbates while sitting on a toilet, especially in the Dutch Reform community that our senator represents. Just as one might sympathize with our ambition for that issue, spearheaded by Lee Montgomery, my assistant and provocateur then, who wished to showcase stories unlike what her workshops offered; and with our industry, rounding up Kathy Acker, John Barth, George Chambers, Robert Coover, Jeffrey DeShell, Rikki Ducornet, Raymond Federman, William H. Gass, John Hawkes, Ben Marcus, Cris Mazza, Ronald Sukenick, David Foster Wallace, Curtis White, and Diane Williams, to name about half the contributors to an issue our university press co-published as a volume of "Innovative Fiction."

And we were a touch smug ourselves, using as a blurb, parallel to praise of the usual sort, the senator's public remark, doubting whether funding such a thing was appropriate use of state money, as we tried to keep writing loose for, with good luck every now and then, another early, sensitive acquisition to art.

I remain grateful to Kostelanetz for his essay on John Cage, in which he quoted Cage as saying, of the work of Joyce, Duchamp, and Eric Satie, that they "resisted the march of understanding

129

and so are as fresh now as when they first were made": that image of the critical enterprise overtaking and grinding the work down with the stomp, stomp, stomp of booted feet, and of art, the worthiest art—experimental art?—resisting such progress, much like the Chinese man who stepped forward in his white shirt to confront tanks rolling toward Tiananmen Square.

Or like an old red wheelbarrow.

"Fragments are inherently poignant, don't you think," Don Justice remarked one warm afternoon, early in a fall semester, and thought to say again when we tried our interview all over one week later, this time with batteries in our recorder.

During that interview, Ed Folsom asked which of the American poets Justice "went back to" most often. "Williams," Don replied, "if I'm looking to learn something."

Sometime or other Gertrude Stein famously said, "It takes thirty years, if you are any good," that long to win recognition, which occurs to me now as I muse on the odd fact that our magazine was the only magazine in America other than the *New Yorker* to have had a selection made from it for *Best American Short Stories, Best American Essays,* and *Best American Poems,* for all three anthologies one year a few years ago, and to have worried, along with happier thoughts, that that may only mean we were doing it all wrong, although two of our selections came from writers entirely new on anyone's chart which means we were doing something right but reminds me, too, of what I often think to say (but have never said) when sending out another rejection, that rather than my feeling apologetic and the writer let down, he or she could take my neglect as a sign of promise.

"I don't think there has been a day in the last ten years," Marilynne remarked, "when I haven't given some thought to Edgar Allan Poe."

Invited to a reading series in a gorgeous room of hardwood and high windows at the New York Public Library, a series in which a magazine would be introduced and would in turn introduce a writer, I invited our Fiction Award winner that year whose story got picked up later by *Best American Short Stories,* and Stellar Kim represented us beautifully with an improbable story about a hesitant romance of an awkward and unlikely middle aged couple, one a cancer patient the other her pathologist. After failing to connect with her while she lived, he bought sexy blue underwear for her laying out at the funeral home. The story was all the more surprising coming from an attractive young woman of whom you might not expect such empathy for the dreary, middle aged. Talking to her beforehand, I learned that her mentor had been Michael Cunningham, on our staff over twenty years before, and that he had promised to attend, which he did. But in the way of New York, Michael was unable to stay for the reception though we managed a nod and a wave as, with a gesture of apology, he slipped out the door.

Sex and censorship, our own, again, a Raymond Carver story: two men out drinking beer and escaping their wives follow two women bicyclists into a park, separate them, and one of the men rapes and murders one of the women, told with a detachment that chilled our readers, especially the women, to whom I deferred, preferring the camaraderie of our reading circle to our relation with Carver, based then on several stories, notably "The Calm" and "View Finder." The latter foreshadows his late, splendid "Cathedral" in the way it calls attention, in dialogue, to that which cannot be said: a man opens his door to a stranger with chrome hooks for hands and asks, right off, "How did you lose your hands." All of which lingers as I second-guess my declining his later rape story.

Recent reviews in *TLS* and elsewhere of books about Aleksandr Solzhenitsyn remind me of a Q & A with Joseph Brodsky after a reading in 1978, the auditorium packed, many of us standing in the aisles, and Brodsky's being baited a little about his countryman who was beginning to appear more a crank than a prophet, possibly worse, an embarrassing fundamentalist, and so the question, "What's your opinion of Solzhenitsyn and the legend that has been built around him?" Brodsky paused, wondering, I imagine, just how far he wanted to go into that before replying, in his angular, high-pitched voice, with its hint of chalk on a blackboard, "Well, let's put it this way, I'm awfully proud that I'm writing in the same language as he does."

Moments later Brodsky recalled Anna Akhmatova's having once said to him that "the only interesting things were metaphysics and gossip."

One spring a college girl coming home from Northwestern wrote to ask whether we might have summer work, which we did not, although if she wished to hang out we would find her a desk, which appealed it seems because she worked faithfully all summer and the image that remains is of her back turned to me and her attention on manuscripts. Once or twice also she babysat for my children, children now grown and parents themselves. Then summer ended and she returned to Northwestern, and that was that until four or five years later I noticed a manuscript submitted by Leslie Pietrzyk, a story with nary a hint in its brief cover letter of any prior acquaintance. "Now that is class," I thought as I read and returned her work without any acknowledgment either while wondering whether this had happened before, how often, and why I had not noticed.

But another story came within a few months, and this time, by responding especially to its closing scene in a southwestern bar where her narrator reacts by thinking, "So this is how to grow up," to tequila and lime, its eye-watering jolt, and to "a thumb rubbing rhythmically against the sideseam of her jeans," we accepted, and found a title for, her new work. Several novels and collections of stories have come out since.

Before her reading at Prairie Lights, Patricia Hampl wondered aloud whether another female MacArthur Award Winner then prominent in our community might show up, but she caught herself just as she let her hope slip and answered of course not, our neighbor would be doing what we should expect. She would be at home at work. Which I remembered at my own first reading, with my new book, when I observed that I'd probably been to at least as many Prairie Lights readings as there were pages in it, and that my book might have been better had I not.

Metaphysics and gossip. Perhaps poetry is the intersection of the two.

"Thinking," replied Wallace Stevens to his daughter's question, "What are you doing, Daddy?" when she found him sitting alone in the dark.

Once Chris Offutt returned his galleys with the request, "Please delete my last sentence," and he was right, and we did, and I heard later—perhaps it's apocryphal—that he had long made it a rule to draft his story completely then cut both the first and last two paragraphs.

A work Harold Bloom marked with his approval, thinking it might resist the march of understanding long enough to survive its century, is *Spanking the Maid* by Robert Coover, which we published as "A Working Day" and that merges sex, experiment, and censorship in its repeated scene of a maid entering a man's apartment, over and over, one morning after another, with his awakening often on display as an erection poorly hidden by his pajamas, then working to tidy the place up until, each time, the man disapproves of her effort and strives to correct her by taking a go at her bottom with a leather belt. His story played on Victorian pornography and *The Story of O* but was a meditation too, as the confrontations of man and maid inched from dawn toward dusk through a working day, a day in a dedicated life, a long day of work, and so on the way a divided self disapproves of and censors its every effort until dissatisfaction with one's work becomes not just "A" but "The" day of work. Coover's first title was accurate. *Spanking the Maid* came later for a separate, letterpress edition that caught Bloom's attention and I'll always wonder whether he would have noticed the earlier title.

Coover's remark on a note that came with final copy of another story—he was "tuning up his sentences" because he'd be spending the next week with William Gass.

A mentor I found in Ann Arbor was hosting a dinner for a visiting lecturer, Caroline Gordon, an aging southern novelist who had twice been married to Allen Tate and so was allied with the all-male, most definitely all-white Fugitives. Robert Hayden was among the guests as was John Aldridge, a well-known critic at that time. Then there were more of us as a supporting cast. It was a late spring, early summer evening as we gathered on the lawn. Do I remember fireflies? I seem to remember fireflies winking along the floral borders, but it also seems early for them. It was warm enough though for Hayden to wear a seersucker suit and dark blue bow tie with his coke bottle glasses. Occasionally I'd find him and Radcliffe Squires, our host, lingering in a stairwell at the university, a quiet place where they could chat; and once I had lingered with them long enough to hear Hayden reflect that the academic life was quite suitable for us, with our bookish ambitions, but he felt guilty about how little it offered our wives. This early evening though, he was lingering with Gordon. She wore a dress that would have shimmered at a tea dance and Hayden looked pretty spiffed up himself. They made an odd couple, the aging southern lady and the in-his-prime black poet, strolling the periphery of the yard head-to-head as if they might soon be holding hands, then settling into a loveseat swing deep in the dusk. That's where I remember the fireflies. Aldridge, meanwhile, who cut the far more cavalier figure, leaned and leaned toward them but never managed to break in.

IV

Serendipity, my Goddess, breaks in now and then, reminding me of Montaigne's observation that "All things are produced by nature, by chance, or by art, the greatest and most beautiful by either of the first two, the least and most imperfect by the last" and so, as Guy Davenport put it, "Imagination is the art of finding things"—his example being arrowheads such as I too have picked up in the fields.

Impossible to know the influence of the farm and seasons, hoping there would be a harvest, with the constant renovation of fields by plowing, disking, and cultivating, loving how the cultivator slices pigweed off between rows of corn, turning the weeds under, turning over fresh earth, pleased with our early summer idiom, also Faulkner's, of "laying the crops by" once they had a strong head start on the weeds, and so accepting the year's cycle which we could have labeled Volume One, Volume Two, on and on as their records went up on a shelf, not to mention the influence of Chaucer, whom I taught year after year, who knew that new corn came out of old fields and the oxen stood awake when he had, once more, a large field to plow.

Long before the postmoderns, Chaucer's self-reflexive narrators interrupted the fictional frame of his text. "I who Love's servants serve," he says of himself, his ardor to his craft transcending that of mere Courtly Lovers in his audience. "Before I walk farther into this tale" he remarks another time, seeing the time and space of his text as tangible elements of his daily life. Then there's his blues couplet, not a couplet exactly, the lines being a page apart, but I'll make it one: "For that oure perche was maad so narwe, allas, / Ful is myne herte of revel and solas!" That's Chauntecleer, perched on a narrow rod in the widow's hall, his grasp on it too insecure for him to reach and "feather" Pertelote.

Impressive the inundation of my desk where manuscripts lie in wait in manila envelopes, and how of a late afternoon the custodian and I are often alone in these halls since he comes around five as I sit benumbed by the opportunities of choice and he sweeps the hall while I dream of clearing my desk, knowing I must reject almost everything on it, with a note whenever I find the words since so many submissions have sat for so long it would be rude to return them as if I had not noticed, the Zen of that as Tom and I pass the time of day and the universe hums around us, radiating down our hall, through my window and out past the library across the parking lot and railroad track, and I make small progress although on occasional afternoons, with a sudden run, I tick seven or ten more off my list of remorse.

My guilt is sometimes tempered by the writer's lack of it for sending such ordinary fare, obvious in feeling, bare in rendering, with no surprise worth the notice, except for the evidence, surprisingly often, of an author's apparent belief that every page he has written deserves a place in some unsuspecting magazine and I should oblige.

"He doesn't have the guts to be a scholar," my old professor snorted. "A scholar is like a poet: you can't stop him." Of course he said, "him." Those were the sixties. But now, neither scholar nor poet, here I am immersed in whatever I've become.

A moment ago a redbird stood watch on the limb in the white pine outside my window, but Titmouse has taken over, swooping down then off to the next limb above with a single sunflower seed from the feeder, which gives Chickadee a chance to dart in and away before Titmouse comes back. How he hammers at his seed, clasped between his toes, his head pecking at it, his tail rising as his head hammers away, the whole of him rocking like an oil field pump, which is when Nuthatch arrives, upside down and aggressive enough to command one side of the feeder, a green-capped, mesh canister which I filled this morning and find half empty already, with Goldfinch clinging now to its rim and taking his time, not one peck and off like Chickadee or Titmouse who dives in as Goldfinch hops to a nearby twig though he's back already once Titmouse flies off with another seed. All are free for the moment of squirrels who dangle down the thin rope that suspends the feeder, a twisted cord less thick than my little finger, clinging to it with their hind feet, head down toward the feeder which they grab and hold, tilting it, spilling seeds, and sating themselves until, dizzy, they jump away, leaving the rest to others. A feeder less than half full offers more to the birds as it attracts fewer squirrels. Though safflower seed is better still since the squirrels wholly reject it, as it took me quite a few years to discover. Now two goldfinches arrive, one male, bright yellow and black, one female, drab, though a reddish headed house finch shared it with the cardinal just moments ago, a cardinal I saw first this morning at my Songbird Café but who

137

has flown off again, as have the finches, though the male has returned and it is hard not to revel in his brilliance though my favorite is Titmouse, jauntily capped, gray, white, with russet on his sides, and whose song—"wheet, wheet, wheet, wheet"— seems his bold announcement that he's coming.

Judith Mitchell, a former assistant for fiction, came to town to read from her first novel, and Thisbe Nissen, one of our readers then, started the questioning by asking about Frank Conroy's rule: "Don't load down your readers' backpacks with anything unnecessary because they will resent lugging the useless up hill," which Judith countered by reminding us of Jim McPherson urging writers to take up what mattered, which might make those backpacks unwieldy, like the ladder on which I had spent much of that summer painting our house, which, when I showed my work off a little proudly at a gathering early in the fall, led Frank to murmur, "anything's easier than writing."

After being asked to direct our MFA Program in Nonfiction, my first visit was to Frank to ask whether any of his staff wanted to share in its teaching—most of them wrote it. "Oh, no, we can't have that," he replied, leaning back in his chair, placing the foot attached to one lanky leg atop the knee of the other and bringing his hands together, his piano-playing hands, fingers spread, finger tips touching. "In fiction you work up the ground as you cross it and never know where you're headed." His hands parted then, their palms turned downward, as if to let the problem roll off toward me. "Nonfiction begins with an outline and you fill it in with prose"—and that from the author of *Stop-Time*. A writer who had not remembered his Montaigne, who remarks that most of his best ideas come while he's on horseback.

I think I garden, or glen as I prefer to say, as Frank would have us write. Dogwood, redbud, shadbush, hemlock, maple, cedar, and yew begin to dot the hillside, something added each year, with something else moved, possibly, from one idea to another, by improvisation and feel, hardly by plan.

When Jim guest-edited an issue of fiction, we found our stories, our favorite—Ethan Canin, my graduate assistant for fiction at the time identified it first—being Peter Nelson's "Cooley and Kedney," the tale of Cooley "F-stop" Fitzgerald, a Zen photographer who planted his seed in the rarest of ways, and of Kedney's "going to Dubuque," her way of singing the blues while she digressed through a decade before accepting Cooley's death-gurney-gift of semen now long frozen and waiting for her. It also involved a train wreck, box cars full of pigs, and the spontaneous combustion of dairy cows, all of which prevented an injured Cooley from getting to the hospital in time, and so his letter to Kedney, as dictated to a nurse, a Vietnamese refugee, wielding a kind of pigeon as Cooley's "endpromptoo stinografer." For years Jim and I smiled about that story and its convoluted escapes whenever we met each other.

Eventually, Jim's memory faltered so that reminding him of his part in such pleasures was like telling him of a person he wasn't sure he knew, though he sounded like a decent fellow.

Nelson modeled Kedney on a girl he had lost, one of my first assistants, who told me her story of coming to Iowa City after dating a man who, having been in the Workshop a few years before, couldn't really object to her getting that chance, although it meant separation, likely for good, but was good enough to drive her to the airport, to see her off, and to agree to transport a trunk of her best things—she mentioned a suede dress—to the bus terminal to follow her here, but who, after seeing her to her plane, dumped her trunk off at Goodwill. "I guess," she said, "I deserved that."

Mary Hussmann and I worked together for a decade and a half during which Carol Bly was a visiting writer which led to Mary's dealing with Bly over an essay, one Mary found fault with and tried to be helpful about but whose advice Bly resisted for who was Mary to advise her? So the essay came to nothing, at least so it seemed, until Bly tried it on a larger magazine somewhere to the east only to get pretty much the same message, which prompted her elegant retreat and recovery as she offered us the essay again, this time following Mary's advice, and acknowledging as much in a note to her saying, "You've got moxie."

An initial idea was to welcome the essay, an inherently experimental form, as little subject to definition as poetry, though there were few recent models and the essay wasn't spoken of as a literary event. There was criticism and my predecessors had christened some few works "Journalit" to hint of a new direction. I knew of Swift, Addison, and Steele and had taught from *The Norton Reader: an Anthology of Expository Prose*. The New Journalism didn't seem quite right—Hunter Thompson hadn't passed my way again either—and the first *Best American Essays* was almost ten years off, so we cast around and came up with a few writings upon which we could bestow the word "essay" as a way of suggesting what we sought.

What is "personal" about the "personal essay" if not its intimate demeanor that infiltrates philosophy to make it tractable, subjective, and shifty. Zones dissolve, boundaries prove permeable, genre is an approximation, and each form we propose—prose poem, lyric essay, personal essay, philosophical tale—can only express a reader's leaning at that moment.

"It's all in the ear of the listener," the jazz-pop-soul singer, Nancy Wilson once said, "Let them decide."

A decision occasioned by the uncertainty of genre was to stop labeling our writings as stories, essays, or poems but to let the reader decide for him or herself, which, though an inconvenience for editors of the several *Best* series, seemed a worthy project, and so we continued for a good many years with the compromising addendum of using those labels anyway in our Annual Index, listing works there as we had assumed we were reading them when we were making our choices.

Lee K. Abbott sent a story with a subtitle, "An Essay on Drink," about which he was adamant, "This is a story, not an essay," and which we loved, and published, and it caught the attention of Robert Atwan, the series editor of *Best American Essays*, who wanted to include it the following year. "Sorry," I replied, it's not an essay," though had I consulted Abbott, he might have relented.

All through my youth, MFA stood for the Missouri Farmers' Association, for seed corn, groceries, and gas, and later for Emma Fay's, a roadside restaurant of the "Good Eats" variety adjacent to an MFA gas station, and it took me I don't know how many years to put MFA together with MFA and bring home a seed cap for Marvin, who favors caps of that kind, and who was appropriately charmed, though the joke wasn't much of one in Iowa.

Maybe I should have brought another for Gerald Stern the afternoon he returned to our screened porch with a lady friend of former years who was miffed at his neglect of her, miffed enough to carefully spill a glass of red wine onto his lap, which only caused Jerry to smile—now that had been got over with—and keep telling stories, such as one about Jack Gilbert who kept asking "how's our book doing," their book being Jerry's *The Red Coal*, which features a photo on its cover of Jerry and Jack strolling the streets of Paris, as Jerry whipped off his pants and asked for a towel and the use of our washer so that by the end of supper, with a little help from Rebecca, he walked off with his lady into the summer night in khakis freshly washed.

Marvin composed the rejection slip I inherited, and its key phrasing explained that "we cannot use" the offering in question and expressed our "regret that the volume of submissions precludes a more personal reply," a phrasing that made me cringe since "we cannot use" obscures our agency of choice and suggests an inability resulting from something like Higher Law, as if we just dropped everything into a hopper, turned a crank and a Natural Law of Evaluation took its course. So after a time I wrote my own note that admitted we read manuscripts in the company of others until we found a few favorites, and that the rejected had thus made an important although "hidden contribution" to our magazine by leading us to what we found we preferred. That only summoned the retort, "hidden contributions" were the least of one's ambitions, thank you very much. Meanwhile I printed Marvin's note on a t-shirt that I couldn't bring myself to wear around town but wore, one winter, on a beach in the Yucatan, and as I passed a couple of vacationers on my way to the water, one man rolled up on his elbows to remark to a friend, "I've got poems there right now."

The morning after we learned that Jorie Graham had won the Pulitzer Prize and there had been a fair hullabaloo as is natural, especially for a town as invested in image and word as this one, I was walking to my office in the English Philosophy Building—sad name for a school as invested in image and word as this one, its Shaker simplicity of meaning ill-married to function on the tongue it clots—the morning cool and the hour early, earlier than my norm for some reason I no longer remember, so that when I approached the Iowa River a mist was rising that the sun ahead of me strove to disperse. Approaching the foot bridge that connects the Memorial Union to the old art building, I could only dimly make out the east side and found the bridge empty but for a young woman just stepping on across the river and walking toward me in the early morning quiet. Her eyes were on the ground, that is on the rusting bridge surface, and I could see that she was wearing a plain gym sweatshirt with tall, emphatic, black lettering that I could not at first make out but saw, as she came nearer, spelled "CHARLES WRIGHT," whose banner she carried west, through the haze of early morning, with nary a glance at me.

The biographical note in most of Strand's books says that he "was born in Summerside, Prince Edward Island, Canada, and was raised and educated in the United States and South America," which I always assumed meant Buenos Aires or Rio, but in a recent Q & A he revealed that as a teenager he had spent six months in Barranquilla, where I spent two years about ten years later. What kind of chance is that?

It was Strand's *Selected Poems* come upon in a library in Nairobi that turned my son on to poetry.

At a stand-up supper before a reading, several of us crowded around John Ashbery, that evening's guest of honor, paper plates and plastic forks in hand, and a colleague, rising to the occasion, said something about Ashbery's being strangely like Robert Frost, which made Ashbery draw back in mock horror, or perhaps real horror, and pronounce that he "hated Robert Frost" but got us to the sestina which he admitted loving—did Frost ever write a sestina? All of which I recalled when I heard Richard Wilbur say he "hated the sestina" although he loved the sonnet, and of those we know several by Frost.

Several years ago, planning to read his book-length poem *Flow Chart* with undergraduates, I wrote Ashbery to see whether he could afford copies of a few manuscript pages so my class might find a foothold in his poem though I was seeking the same, wary of depending too much on my impromptu way with a class hour. Soon I received a call from one of his assistants asking whether I had a particular portion of the poem in mind which left me nonplussed since I had barely read it myself and felt, in the peculiar way Ashbery's poems have of making me feel that I must read it all over again, and that it would seem just as unfamiliar a second time, which is a compliment *à la* Cage I would guess.

"What about the double sestina," his assistant asked, which made my mind spin like a bike tire on loose gravel since I had not noticed a single much less double sestina anywhere in the book though I had made a marginal note, "lots of sunflowers here," which might have tipped me off. "Sure," I replied, "that would be fine" and soon received a photocopy of thirty-nine pages, long lines, single spaced, each page filled from side to side, the whole of it marked "first complete typescript" and comprising at least the last third of *Flow Chart*, within which I found that double sestina as well as a lovely run on the avant-garde that picks you up and sets you down elsewhere, not where you had intended to go but where it felt perfectly right to have arrived, a congenial conundrum for which the likeness was a bicycle race through the countryside of France. Then as I turned pages, wider and wider eyed, I discovered one had been left out of his book completely, one whole typescript page, top line through bottom, the bottom line of the page before joined to the top line of the page after—and the passage from one to the other as smooth as coasting down a sloping lane in gentle Languedoc.

Roses for the typist who by turning over two pages together, not noticing that she had, and typing right on, demonstrated how "everything connects," as Ashbery put it during an informal Q & A the morning after his reading in answer to Jorie's asking what one philosophical idea he found the most persuasive.

When Paul Engle brought Czeslaw Milosz to read in Iowa City, it was a humid midsummer Saturday afternoon in an auditorium on the edge of downtown with its several cafés at one of which Milosz lunched with the Engles, a lunch that stretched on as the auditorium filled with late comers perching on the steps of both aisles and the weather warm and the air conditioning inadequate but most persons patient, though some dabbed themselves with handkerchiefs and kept looking for ceiling fans when Milosz strode in alone, fifteen minutes past the hour, wearing gray slacks, blue blazer, white shirt and tie, and picked his way over people filling the aisle all the way down to the front where he climbed on stage and took a seat beside a small wooden table with a glass of water beside which he placed a couple of books then crossed his legs, folded his hands, and sat as we wondered who was being held up, how and why, and our waiting stretched on, marked by an old wooden clock with a minute hand that swung a minute ahead with a small click every sixty seconds until Milosz, impatient, or sympathizing with us as that hand hit the twenty-five minute mark and the temperature rose in a room increasingly packed, rose himself and stepped to the podium where he began to introduce his own reading. "I am Czeslaw Milosz; I have come from Berkeley to be with …" at which precise moment the door in the back thudded open and Engle strode in, stumbling over persons backed against it, and Milosz continued with but a nanosecond of pause (though we did not use that word then), "my good friend, Paul Engle, whom I have the honor of introducing to you," which made Engle whoop and all but float down the aisle as Milosz continued with a few words on their friendship and Engle hurried through a refreshingly brief introduction before turning the room back over to a master.

V

After the flood of 2008, after exile from our offices yet getting our August issue out on time from temporary quarters in an upper hallway of a building on high ground, I thought, "Let's do a River Issue" and stumbled again upon a chief pleasure of this work—initiating an idea without need for anyone's approval. The idea is foundation, the rest construction: mentioning it to others, paying attention where it resonates, prodding likely sources, inviting writers for their special experience or knowledge, a few of whom might not have thought of themselves as contributors; finding the chance here and there to extend the thought as metaphor, letting art that was not intended as a depiction of river be seen as such, even a long, flowing sound-poem, something like extended scat singing, be offered as an "articulation of river." Joining in the enthusiasm awakened among contributors, letting that lead to the photographic archives of the State Historical Society in one instance, to panel sessions of a conference in another, then seeing our staff rise to the challenge of integrating unusual art, wrestling unwieldy material into shape, and working steadily until, as another summer careens toward August, the issue comes into our hands and we are immersed in our next project.

Priscilla Sears spent a year in China, teaching writing and encouraging her students "to find their own voice," as was our idiom then, something formulaic to say about what appeared to be the first successful slim volume of verse by a young poet.

Not that anyone knew how, but we believed—such were our clichés—that doing so, in first-year composition as in poetry, was the important action, liberating, self-determining, and personally empowering, as we liked to say. The most distinctive characteristic of Sears' students, however, wasn't "voice" but determination. With lights out at ten in their dorms—barracks would be more like it—they stood under dim street lamps, in the cold, reading Milton. Those are students I would remember and whom I thought of again, years later, when I met Yiyun Li. They have a certain presence with me after years. At least my memory of Sears' essay sticks. But they were mystified by her urging them to find their own voices: "Why would we want to do that?" they inquired.

The four most important American poets?—Joseph Brodsky, Seamus Heaney, Derek Walcott, and Czeslaw Milosz, Marvin remarked with a smile in the early 80s before even one had won the Nobel Prize.

Unlike some colleagues, I have never been in wont of a topic and for over three decades have always known what counted for work, a discipline I never expected, my Zen of Attention, going to the office far more days than not, checking the mail, sorting and filing some of it, answering a few inquiries that could be answered quickly, reading manuscripts, writing notes, writing an acceptance letter every once in a while, looking ahead in our Running Table of Contents and juggling as needed to make the pages come out, returning manuscripts, a few with comments, or, as the rhythm of production calls for it, sharing in the proofreading and lay-out of an issue, dividing the writing by genres and then each genre into smaller groups, rotating and placing those groups to point up pleasing juxtapositions, then trimming the self-advertisements of our Contributors' Notes before finding an order on the back cover for the names of our writers with attention to sound, rhythm, and available rhymes—the found poem of names by which, for several years, we ended issues. Then reading the whole all over again as the last reader before sending it to press, calling or emailing writers when I stumbled over a problem we should have noticed earlier but had allowed ourselves not to find critical until that last moment, checking the bluelines and the color match for the cover and thumbing the uncut pages before one day receiving a box with twenty-four copies of a new issue by which time we are into producing our next with two or three more lined up in our files, perhaps with a hole or two in each for which I return to my special shelf, often finding notes from Lynne on the envelopes since she would have read most of them already.

Barranquilla was a happy accident, and when it was time to come home, I wrote Fredson Bowers at Virginia and got a letter back quickly, asking a few questions which I answered, and he wrote again asking more and so back and forth several times, while I was unaware that he was a collector and his questions were prompting more and more bright floral stamps. The more third world the country the more gaudy the stamp I once thought some kind of law. Finally Bowers had teased enough out of me and, being a gentleman, gave in, saying, "Your grades aren't quite what we're looking for and you're in this godforsaken place where you can't take the exams we require, but why don't you come give grad school a try? I'll try to find you some sort of gradership."

Walking home now I pass a bronze sculpture in the form of a stack of five books, the top one lying open so its spread pages shelter the other four from sparrows and pigeons, rain, snow, and the ash of cigarettes. And there it is, my name on the spine of one of those books. Mine is the thinnest of its stack, a modest book, but the representation of a book nevertheless, so I have a place in a "literary walk" in a city well aware of its heritage. My election to this modicum of renown has more to do with the three decades I spent editing *The Iowa Review* than with the few books I have written myself. That is notable, that an editor should be included, and I do not complain. It is an odd gesture though, all of it. Intended as a way of celebrating and keeping in mind persons and work connected to our town, it is equally a promise of oblivion. Ozymandiases in our infancy are we all. Who was he, or she, I already ask of names I pass. It's like scanning the Tables of Contents of old literary magazines and noting the unknowns who kept company with the few we remember, so far. Attendant courtiers we are, swelling the scene and so contributing to the compost from which new work emerges.

The Fayum portraits were made to place on mummies of Egyptian dead, and those mummies, with the remarkable likenesses of the mummified pasted on them, some as haunting in their dark, fine looks as if Caravaggio were the painter, as we learned from the volume of reproductions that Stavros once sent us, stood propped in corners of their homes until they were no longer recognized. Then they were pitched in some North African midden.

Richard Howard speaking of his "favorite poet," Anonymous: "Would you publish your poems anonymously," a listener asked. "Well, yes," Howard replied, "if everyone else would."

"Rhyme" went up on the blackboard and "rhythm," "sound," "music," "meter," "image," and "voice," a "personal voice," one that sounds "intimate." There was no fixed answer, only components of a possible one down the line somewhere for an honors seminar called "The Origins of the English Lyric." The question was what were the essential elements of lyric poems and our list was promising although without surprise. Then a young woman, quiet so far, said "juxtaposition." There was a voice from a different quarter, with a word for a different list.

She might have learned from "Western Wind," by Anonymous, a poem I strove to make iconic all that semester: "… the smalle raine downe can raine / Christ that my love were in my arms…" But Tara may have known already and brought her word from somewhere else.

Another time when Strand was in town, I sat in the back of the room admiring his sport coat, sport coats being a weakness of mine, only to discover, when I joined the lunch table later, that I owned the same jacket. I'd found mine on sale at Saks ten years before and I too still wore it. But that's when I heard him say, after ruminating on how he thought he had finally learned how to teach Kafka, that he never felt more like a poet than when he was writing prose.

Had he not moved on from Barranquilla so soon, Thompson might have joined Ignacio and me on our trip to Ciénaga, directly north of Aracataca, the boyhood home of Gabriel García Márquez, and a model for Macondo in its small town state. This was five years before *One Hundred Years of Solitude* was published so for most of us those towns did not yet exist when Ignacio's uncle, who would have been a boy at the crucial time, escorted me to the station and described the massacre of banana workers who had dared strike against the United Fruit Company and told how their bodies had been removed from town by rail. Dusk was gathering, several boxcars stood on a siding open and empty and I could all but hear the pulse of a train pushing through. But my Spanish was sluggish, Ignacio cared more about a cousin and her girlfriends—we'd be dancing the *cumbia* in dusty streets soon—so even though my host's agitation was vivid, death trembled in his telling, and my country was deeply involved, by the special poignancy of art, my host had to wait on García Márquez for his story to become real.

Thompson had a special directness, a getting-right-to-it, typing out *The Great Gatsby* and *A Farewell to Arms* sentence by sentence to learn the feel of a classic. Just as, whether or not it was she, he knew the image of the girlfriend he wanted us to know he had. And I've long wondered, whether with his nose for a story, he would have sniffed this sour one out, with hardly any Spanish, and what he might have made of it.

One of the most impressive things about poetry as an art is how it blends with poetry that is not, but that is not not-poetry either. A man's wife dies and suddenly, inexplicably, he writes poetry. He reads poetry, too, and attends poetry readings. Only poetry, of all the world's attractions, holds his attention and poems are what he writes, rhymed or unrhymed, in lines that avoid the margins—in more senses than one—but with daring amounts of white space to articulate unaccountable whispers, silences, and juxtapositions, some of which might have resonated with those Chicago school children. This is not prose though most likely we find it "unpublishable," and so our printed slips that apologize for "not being able to use it," by which we finesse the personal responsibility we take for assuming as much. For there is nothing unpublishable about it if we decide otherwise. No vigilantes of verse would appear to extract the offender from our pages.

Tim McGinnis grew up in north central Illinois to become a writer in New York from where he sent us a three-page story, "The Trail," that imagined Kafka as a distracted hiker at Boy Scout Camp. We loved his wry tale and placed it first in an issue, to learn, a couple of years later, that McGinnis, barely thirty, had died of a brain tumor. The news came when his family approached us to sponsor an award in his name for he had been especially pleased by our acceptance of his work, over the transom as the saying goes, what we are most here for when we are at our best.

It was Jim McPherson, or Valerie Lagorio, or Norman Sage who nominated Rebecca and me for The Feques, that is the Not Fequeless—we have a certificate to prove it—and to join the three of them and Ellie Simmons for visits to Norman by the lake with a luncheon we'd cater ourselves, all this, in part, as a way of checking up on Norman, then in his eighties, who continued to write stories. He put one hand on his lap, palm up, and raised the other higher than his shoulder, palm down, to answer how many, and eventually *Waiting for the Fireworks* came out, with a little help from Jim and me and from Mary who is not otherwise in this story. It became a question though who, Norman or his dog Beauregard, would outlast the other, and a pleasure to visit with Jim, away from the university. He always drove Ellie out, at about twenty miles an hour, while we brought Valerie, both of them gone now, and Norman, and Beauregard, and more recently, Jim, leaving Rebecca, Mary even if she's not in this story, and me; and if we go down in order as we mostly have so far; well, I am oldest.

Norman published his own chapbooks, *Lover Go Back to Him, Tuesday at Nine, In the Valley of Nagging Doubts, Unprovoked Assaults on Old Loves, Loitering with Intent, Hate, Hate II,* and other amiable titles, under the names, Hooper Thorne, C. J. Cooley, Jack Hammer, and Gladwyn Thrush, among others. I found his pamphlets endearing for their occasional blunders and for his spare aesthetic, austerity with a wink, governed by the labor of setting his own type. So I put in a selection once, under the name Hooper Thorne, wherein music was "stuff that uses up /

a lot of notes, / and if you are good at it, / you are a very special person, / but if you are not / you are just one of the guys."

Jim Barnes, a recent McGinnis Award winner, mentioned the thrill of the "big littles," a category in which he included us. "There is nothing," he said, "quite like publishing in a big little magazine" and knowing your work has been chosen from hundreds of competing possibilities, knowing, that is, that you have held the disinterested attention of peers and may pirouette briefly on the stage they have set. The sense of community in that, its loose knit association of sympathies, keeps writers writing and their work flowing to us so that I spent much of several decades feeling guilty toward those for whom I failed to muster quite enough sympathy, much less found a way of wedging into our pages.

At conferences, the real question, no matter how disguised, is "How do I get into your magazine," which I've found impossible to answer though I did tell once of Jim the Wonder Dog, who lingers in the lore of my hometown where he died in the 1930s and was buried just outside the cemetery, though the cemetery has expanded since then so that now Jim's grave is at its center and the most visited site therein. For Jim was a remarkable dog, intelligent, prescient, able not only to identify from a ring of observers in the lobby of the local hotel the visitor, the doubter, the traveling salesman with the out-of-state car, or the woman who came wearing her sister's red dress, but who predicted the outcome of presidential elections and of the Kentucky Derby for seven straight years, at least so it is said. All this began on a quail-hunting trip when his master grumbled, "It's hot Jim, why don't you find us the shade of an old walnut?" Forget for a moment that walnuts are indifferent shade trees. Jim did and the questions never stopped, to the point of tedium if you ask me since there's only so much to be squeezed from identifying again an unfamiliar license plate or familiar red dress. But if Jim had been asked to locate yet another walnut on another hot afternoon and had balked until back in the hotel but then marched across the lobby to stand before a fine breakfront cabinet—that I hope I would always recognize as work to accept.

Years ago I worked with a graduate student who wanted to write a master's thesis about Thompson and had arranged to meet him in Florida and had driven south to do so only to be stood up but, being indefatigable, made the date all over again, this time for Aspen and devoted his Spring Break to the trip, to be stood up once more though he did spend an evening chatting with the bartender in Thompson's favorite bar and came home to write a thesis on Not Meeting Hunter Thompson.

So Indie rock bands, a veteran tells me, prepare demos to send out, by email these days, then wait a week or two before checking to see whether the package arrived by leaving inquiries "on a phone that no one ever picks up," too embarrassed all the while to go out to the club only to find the booker at the bar just waiting to laugh at the pathetic band that had tried to beg its way in. Where you've played and with whom are essential factors of a rock 'n' roll resume, and if the booker fails to say "yes," you try and try again and I wonder where musicians found the pattern for such peculiar behavior?

Oriole just turned up in the pine outside my window and alerted me with a single strike of his bell, as round and full and orange as his breast. It's a perfect rhyme, the sliced orange he savors with the color he wears. I recognize his note instantly after months of his absence, and since I had half an orange out for him, pinioned on a redbud twig, he seemed to know to say thanks. Catbirds too arrived a few days ago in this season when everyone is staking out territory for themselves, the wren and hummingbird other recent arrivals, flying such distances, by gorgeous maps ingrained, "instinct" we call it, reluctant to credit them with understanding and knowledge, although what we write and send around and are pleased to have published might just be another way of finding our way home and ringing our bell.

If magazines are fragile adumbrations of books in their becoming, they are more fragile than ever these days as one after another of even the "big littles" goes down, or off, off the field we have shared, and in some cases on, that is online, a turn that may prove neither terrible nor tragic but is a turn nevertheless from the tangible, the tactile, the coordination of many tasks that have long taxed me so that a fresh object, very like a book, comes into your hands, a contemporary codex, this moment's inheritor of a tradition of making and transmission at least two millennia long, this old/new wonder to open once more, the carrier of many small touches of word and design to be noticed by whoever notices.

Put X people together for Y months and a magazine will emerge, inevitably.

Every issue a "sallying out," a "little light attack" as Montaigne put it—an essay, one after another after another.

It took me years to interpret these rings and layers of devotion, not just to our magazine but to many like it, by unknown writers who keep writing, by well known writers who send too, by the faithful band, dozens now, who never said "No," when asked to serve as a judge for our annual awards, and the staff, some paid a pittance with RA stipends, others wholly volunteer who come to meetings, read new work, argue for selections, proofread and proofread more, and me too sticking with it so. Where does the love come from for I must call it that, and I think I know: it is the obverse of and complementary to the commitment required of a writer; it is the pull of community finding its balance with a writer's need to draw into one's self and into one's work; it is the belief, deep down, so subterranean as to be subliminal, that the writing actually does matter more than the writer.

It's a cottage industry, for those who love cottages.

VI

A squirrel just chewed off a small branch and carried it high in the pine beside my window, and now is back for another, which he, or she, grabs by the butt end, where she chewed it off, then, using her forepaws, shifts her mouth's grip on it, centering the branch for better balance or to keep it from snagging on a limb or twig as she scrambles up the trunk to her nest-under-construction and now comes for a third branch in the time it's taken me to type this much, no a fourth since he dropped the first one I saw him chew off. Amazing the things I know nothing about that are right in front of me, and have always been, squirrels, perhaps two of them running relays up a pine trunk with twiggy branches in their mouths, deft little makers that they are.

Right in front of me, and left there too. Old branches and new, for me to pick up.

It must have been in college, with days of wandering to the newsstand, scanning the paperbacks, and to the library with its shelf of new arrivals, nearly all of which had been checked out and maybe even read by T. Baird, one of my professors and a fierce one. "Mr. Johnson," I overheard him exclaim to a classmate, "you would be a better writer if you were a different man," which is not that much a surprise once you think about it. And to a periodical reading room where recent issues of magazines were laid out for browsing, where I found the *Critical Quarterly* and *Hudson Review,* the latter with writing by professors I had so that, for the first time, I could attach faces to names in literature, no matter how marginal, men I might pass on the street in their charcoal suits and thin ties, though one did affect a denim work shirt under his tweed sport coat, a shirt like my father wore in the fields, although my prof set off his with a gold collar pin. I earned C's and B's from him and his mates, my only A coming from that same T. Baird, but that is another story.

It was a Shakespeare class for which we read one play a week and ended each week with a quiz that always asked a few brief questions to warm up our close-reading skills before posing one that probed what we thought Shakespeare was really up to in our play of the week to which I answered, the first time out, remembering Baird's holding up a skull like Yorik's to stress Shakespeare's unbridgeable distance from us, that though this or that idea was attractive, maybe even clever, I would not presume "to know" what was "on the mind" of genius. So I earned my A, my reward for humility, or for plain commonsense, or for cheekiness since it would be hard to tease all that apart. And I learned to invent a variant of my answer quiz after quiz, which kept the A's coming and led me to ask Baird two years later for a recommendation to graduate school as my time in Barranquilla was coming to a close, which must have helped since I found myself soon at one of the two universities to which I applied.

It probably helped, too, that Baird and Bowers had been at Harvard at about the same time where both had been students of Kittredge, whose text they assigned and whose glosses Bowers wanted us to memorize. All of which I surmise not just from their both assigning that text, a streamlined *Complete Works* compared to what we have now, but from a peculiar, gawky gesture both had, as if a tongue depressor serving as a horizontal exclamation point had stretched their mouths wide and pulled their eyes down into a squint, to the point of farce had we had the courage to laugh. Grimaces I can only explain as variants of the same master text, with Kittredge its probable author.

"Just because you can say it doesn't make it so," my old professor added on another afternoon, unable to see his remark as a goad for much of his century's writing, philosophical, critical, and imaginative. And this time I'll add it was Bowers.

Now I can stick my finger just about anywhere in the long run of the *Review* and, after rifling a little, pull out some sort of plum. Say Volume 33, No. 1, Spring 2003. Here are the contributors' names on the back cover:

> Deborah Tall, Oliver Rice, Russell Scott Valentino,
> Anthony Swofford, Ilan Stavans, Caroline Barry,
> Leonard Kress, Melanie Jordan Rack, Joe Cislo,
> Jill Osier, Lyall Bush, Chimamanda Ngozi Adichie—

Stories upon stories and poems. Knowing Tall since she was an undergraduate at Michigan. Finding Valentino as our next editor, a transition editor as it turned out. Having found Stavans in other magazines, but never before hosting him in ours. Swofford, *Jar Head,* and the year he was our assistant for fiction. Osier, some Iowa connection that I know nothing more of. And the *ab* pattern begun, long o, long e, repeat. More of a stretch, but more intriguing, given the names entering our culture, like Chimamanda Ngozi Adichie, a name we're not even sure how to pronounce.

> Sean Singer, Ann Struthers, I.Y. Hashimoto,
> Matthew Lippman, Christine Deavel, Zona Teti,
> Chris Offutt, John Samuel Tieman, Stephen Lowe,
> Rick Bursky, Kathleen Flenniken, Nick Moudry,

Not just the rhymes, but the rat-a-tat-tat of Tieman, Offutt, Teti. Offutt's was the story from which we cut the last sentence. Teti, a poet whose poem, an earlier poem, I once featured in an essay though I've never met her. And Christine Deavel, whom I barely knew some twenty years ago when we printed a poem I've never forgotten. We hadn't heard from her again until now. Here is her earlier poem.

On Top of a Small Porch

> a boy shinglewalks. He tries the slant
> almost to the eaves. He wiggles his fingers
> in the air above the redbud and the car,
> thinking that tonight when he sits on the porch
> with his family, he will look up
> and see himself not touching the wall.
> His big father is settled in the window
> over the roof. They are so close that the distance
> is almost wonderful. So the father, wearing
> the undershirt, after work, is calm.
> His thick hands rest loose in his lap, while over
> and over he sings to this boy in the baggy pants—
> "Come in, come in, come in Roof King."

Of course it's that last line. So simple and unexpected. The parents' quiet, yet awed celebration of their boy becoming a lad. Other touches to admire. The "big father" with "thick hands." The first phrase unusual though made of the most common words. The father sitting "so close" at an "almost wonderful" distance. Then, especially, the parent imagining that the boy sees himself not touch the wall. "Roof King" has come back to me at unexpected moments over a good many years. I was very glad to host Deavel again with another, quietly strange poem that I won't go into.

Meanwhile the rhymes continue, with a pair of couplets to close it off, the rhymes exact to the ear even if surprising to the eye.

Daniel J. Langton, Kathryn Starbuck, Joshua Kryah,
James DenBoer, Jerry Harp, Steve Tomasula,
Lance Olsen, Pappi Tomas, Sunshine Gladstone,
Rand Richards Cooper, Laura Nichols, Ada Limón

Why bother with the name-poem? No real reason. Just one of those small tactile touches that made another issue feel complete and in some sense ours, including as it does in this instance another former staff member, two actually, both poetry assistants, one using a pseudonym that rhymes with Limón, new to us in this issue, without yet having had a book out, and who was just announced as the 2018 winner of the National Book Critics Circle Award for poetry.

But Chimamanda Ngozi Adichie. It's not that we knew to feature her. If anything, as far as fiction headliners went, we put Anthony Swofford and Chris Offutt up front as a pair that made sense to us and to others, and later, a contrasting duo, Lance Olsen and Steve Tomasula, as counterweights in the issue. Neither Tomasula nor Olsen were first time with us either. Both were, in a sense, old friends.

But even then, amongst all this, and it had to have been in 2002, maybe late 2001, something about Chimamanda Ngozi Adichie caught us. She rose from the slush. Perhaps it was Hugh Ferrer who paused over her story first, or Ted Genoways, or Paula Morris, visiting from New Zealand, Megan Levad, still an undergrad honors student, or Margaret Schwartz, who would be off soon to Argentina to translate Macedonio Fernández. All were reading fiction with us then. Maybe Hugh, who was helping with the International Writing Program, took a special interest in an African name.

Adichie's first novel, *Purple Hibiscus*, had yet to appear. A second, *Half of a Yellow Sun*, won the Orange Prize in 2006 and marked her for international renown. But we had no knowledge of that yet, nor of what followed: a visiting appointment to Princeton, a MacArthur Award, a Ted Talk, and a National Book Critics Circle Award in 2013 for her novel *Americanah*. Chimamanda Ngozi Adichie became a star. If the Swedes ever get around to awarding Nobel Prizes in literature again, her name will appear on several lists.

But we didn't know any of that. We just sparked to a story told from the point of view of a young Nigerian woman sent to the states as the bride of an apparently successful Nigerian doctor already here. It was an arranged marriage. The story begins with a young woman's introduction to the doctor's sad apartment and soon the weight, in several senses, of a husband on her, a weight for which she is supposed to be grateful.

> "Look around, look around. You get used to things faster that way," he said. I turned my head from side to side so he would see that I was looking around.

Her taking a casual expression literally helped—you almost laugh—and a simile, about to appear, did no harm.

> Dark restaurant windows promised the Best Caribbean and American Food in lopsided print, a car wash across the street advertised $3.50 washes on a chalk board nestled among Coke cans and bits of paper. The sidewalk was chipped away at the edges, like something nibbled by mice.

It's not that we discovered Adichie, at least not all alone. And we could have helped her a little by moving her phrase, "in lopsided print." We don't catch everything. But we were among the first to publish her work, and she has given us credit for that. As she might. Someone here was paying attention, and being accepted by one of the "big littles" has been known to open doors. Therefore, a few years later, when we were asked to supply a pair of readers for an evening at Housing Works, a non-profit bookstore in New York, we asked Adichie to represent us, and she graciously accepted. We paired her with Marvin Bell who, fortunately, was going to be in New York that week. A terrific event for us, bringing two stars to that program.

About the same time, Yiyun Li appeared. She had been working with Jim McPherson, who urged me to admit her to our Nonfiction Writing Program. She joined my first course on Montaigne. "Ideas enough here for a lifetime," Yiyun burst out one afternoon, winning the assent of her new friend and writing companion, Amy Leach. They still share their work. Amy ended our program by making a conference presentation that led Albert Goldbarth, who followed her on stage, to exclaim, "she's like a cross between Tim Burton and Emily Dickinson." I.e., "from outer space" as Marvin likes to say.

"Bell stands at an odd angle with the universe," suggested one of his reviewers, and Marvin asked me what I thought that meant, and I was able to say, having just found the book alluded to in my favorite secondhand bookstore. E. M. Forster said it of Cavafy in an essay on Alexandria and that meant good enough. "Differently wired" is another of his expressions about our odder students, a few of whom disturb us as Emily D disturbed Higginson.

Montaigne I had no authority to teach. He was just worth reading, especially by MFA students in nonfiction, and no one else in the university offered a course. Through Chaucer, not quite two hundred years before him, and Shakespeare, about half a century after, I could catch Montaigne in a kind of triangulation. That was enough for a start; then we could read together and soon find him saying, of Cicero, "Moreover I do not know how

162

to excuse him for having considered his poetry worth being published." That's in "Of Books."

Here's Marvin's succinct recipe for learning to write: "Read something, then write something; read something else, then write something else. And show in your writing what you have read." Because, as he adds: "A poem listens to itself as it goes."

"'This isn't written, as the French say,' said Plekhenov, turning back Lenin's slapdash polemic." So Russell Fraser began, quoting Plekhenov who was quoting the French. "But Lenin," Fraser adds, "focused on content, didn't know what his editor was talking about."

"It's not about content," Marvin often adds. Thus Jorie, it's not experience, it's "the sentence."

More recently, Brian Dillon: "you will have failed as it were to *write while writing.*" He's trying to describe the same need of listening to oneself, which isn't new; that was Montaigne's expertise, not to mention the bookworm-riddler's.

Probably the Haida elder on my first page knew that a real teller with a tale to tell would be one who tells her own telling.

Say as a slugger, you lift a high fly ball and hope to make a double of it. You tear down the base path with your eye on the defenders, on the coach at first base, and on the ball. You can't watch it, but you must keep an eye on it, or you just might be picked off.

Am I going to trip over "tear"? Then what about "trip?"

Donald Hall's term for such usage was "dead metaphor." He hated them. What about keeping your eye on the ball? It's less a dead metaphor, more a marvel, when you don't but do.

Over the summer I've noticed that titmice come more and more rarely, so rarely that I thought they had moved on, or had fallen prey to neighborhood cats, but once in a while, after an interval of weeks, I would see a pair again though their appearances thin through August to virtually never, and my progressive rationing of the seed so squirrels and sparrow squadrons are less attracted can't be the whole answer since Nuthatch, Chickadee, and House Finch still show. I have decided that titmice, more resourceful than others, need me less, though I keep an eye out for them, loving their quick movement, jaunty cap and dark eyes. They have become my Emblem of Choice, the rarest at the feeder though still in the neighborhood as I discovered again when I heard "Wheet, wheet, wheet, wheet" a moment ago and noticed a family of four browsing the high limbs of a hackberry.

Here's Creeley covering Hardy. The poem is called "Versions." He keeps his eye on Hardy, as he admits in his epigraph, while writing his poem.

> . . . and why the pain still,
> the pain—
> still useless to them—
>
> as if to begin again—
> again begin—
> what had never been?

Maybe someday I'll understand why such passages sing to me. His ear is on Hardy, that too.

Perhaps the ultimate value of all this work for me: the *Review*, working with "real writers," gave me a certain authority in the classroom, especially classrooms filled with aspiring writers. At the same time, conversely, and more or less equally, all that teaching of Chaucer, Shakespeare, and Montaigne gave me a certain confidence as a reader of real writers. Then again there were the students and student-assistants who often ran ahead and showed me.

In a later paper that semester, the student who thought "juxtaposition," quoted from a rejection slip that came to Sylvia Plath: "After a heavy rainfall, poems titled 'Rain' pour in from across the nation." Well, yes, "pour," but that was some other editor's problem. Tara though adds, "I find this an amusing comment on how screening a lyric impulse is part of learning to say something new."

"Revelations come when they come," wrote another student, "and are sometimes prompted by sugar."

During our bicentennial year when I was new to Iowa, two years before I took over the *Review,* Matthew Pollard, a biology major in an undergraduate writing class, imagined fishing the Iowa River—but way off in the future, in the dimly imaginable year, 2000. By then, Matthew assumed, pollution would have forced us to live under constant alert—Don't Eat Fish From This River! Nevertheless, the siren joys of fishing would still sing to us, so the state had established nurseries upstream for raising trout, walleye, and bass. When game fish matured, they were slaughtered by electric shock, packaged in cellophane, and dropped in the river. And, since dead fish float belly-up, nursery workers would attach a loop to the belly of each packaged fish so a fisherman, wielding an elongated pool cue with a small brass hook on its end, could lift his catch from the stream. Matthew pictured a legion of old men lined up on the riverbank near the English Philosophy Building, taking stab after stab at fish passing beneath the Iowa Avenue Bridge.

Well, he wasn't quite on target. Those catfish I lugged home and feasted on without mishap were handed to me about the time Matthew projected. But I carried them home thinking of his warning, which has only become more pointed.

Just now Rebecca wondered whether I intended those cellophane-wrapped dead fish to signify manuscripts that float in over our transom. "Not exactly," I replied, "not consciously anyway." But there is something in us that longs to fish even when we take home little or nothing. Or watch birds, I will add, remembering that very old story of the 5th day when fish and birds came into being together. I've found my favorites among them, too, and haven't even got yet to kestrels, not a bird of our backyard, but one whose flair I've long kept an eye out for when driving our highways and byways.

Charlottesville

James Alan McPherson joined our faculty in the early 1980s. I'd learned of Jim several years before through his first book, *Hue and Cry*. A story from his second collection, *Elbow Room*, had appeared in *The Iowa Review* before I became its editor. Now I wanted to meet him. I knew we were about the same age, and it seemed likely that we could become friends. One way to achieve that would be to work side by side. Jim was coming as a recent Pulitzer Prize winner and a MacArthur Fellow. He was in the first group awarded MacArthur Fellowships. It would be a coup to enlist him as Guest Editor for a special issue of fiction.

Jim agreed, but he had a condition. He didn't want to go it alone; he wanted me to work up the issue with him. That meant meeting together to cull our selections from the two, three, or four dozen stories that arrived unsolicited every week. We had a student assistant; that year it was Ethan Canin. He and Jim met regularly. But finally it came down to Jim and me going over our gleanings and deciding which stories would compose our issue. It took me awhile to catch on, but this proved Jim's way of finding me out.

We preferred to get out of our offices and chose the River Room, a cafeteria in the student union across the street from our building. It had a long view of the river that runs through our campus and town. Crowded over the noon hour, it usually emptied out by two. We could always find a table with a view and with room to spread out manuscripts under consideration.

In hindsight, our meetings resembled that storied psychoanalytical hour when, after forty minutes of dancing around and avoiding the issue, you finally get down to business for the final ten. It is always possible, however, and even likely, that the real business came and went, perhaps not well observed, during those first forty minutes.

We made most of our selections during the final fraction of the hour or so we spent together. The greater portion of our time was like a slow, formal dance. Jim had come from Charlottesville where he had not been happy. In fact he swore never to return. Twenty years before, as a graduate student, I had found it more than comfortable. Jim's home was Savannah, Georgia, a segregated city in a segregationist state. I grew up in rural Missouri, a border state with overwhelmingly Confederate sympathies. At its university, which I did not attend, and at UVA, fraternities waved the rebel flag at football games; and though I found that tactless, I had not overtly disowned it. We had both gone to segregated grade schools and high schools, although integration came to my school while I attended, and it came peacefully. Not many generations before, however, there had been lynchings in my county, at least three I knew of. I never asked how many Jim knew of in and around Savannah. We had both spent a few years in Massachusetts, and that conjunction worked in our favor. I had also spent one long autumn at an artists' retreat a twenty-minute boat ride from Savannah. I had loved my time on that island and in myriad small ways had prospered from it. Jim never mentioned having been there, and an invitation, such as I had been handed, would, most likely, never have come. Nor, not being a swimmer, would he have relished the boat ride out to the island. My Savannah was far from his Savannah. I had much to answer for.

Our dance was a test; Jim was testing how far he could trust me. A kind of twinned mythologizing took place as we lay our stories down, side by side, not just once but, with variations and improvements, every time we met. Of course our stories were disjunctive. But they were complementary. Jim led and I followed, and it took me several sessions to realize we were going to swing through these moves, with variations, each time.

Jim told of his father who had been the first licensed African American electrician in Georgia, but who also landed in jail. Then of abuse from a grade school teacher because his father was a con. He told also of submitting his first stories to a contest while in college and discovering the instructor, whose signature was required, had failed to pass his work on. Then how, in the following year, he got around that professor and got his work submitted. That led to his meeting his first editor, in Boston, a man who took him out to lunch and coached him, among other things, not to write "motherfucker" more than a very few times. He always smiled telling me that.

Much else that Jim told me you can find in the stories and essays he has written, and it is not my place to retell them. I of course had to keep the conversation going without having written my share of stories, much less prize-winners. But I told of my rural background in Missouri, my father and uncle clearing bottomland and developing a farm and of the odd chance that I would have been accepted at Amherst College in the late 50s—a white kid from a small Missouri town—in an early effort at diversity.

Charlottesville was a more delicate topic. Jim had gone through a divorce there and felt ill-treated. A few years later, as we got to know each other better, he asked me to write a character reference to the court where an adjustment to the decision was pending. In any event, I did, eventually, get around to admitting that my own time in Charlottesville had been pleasant, insofar as graduate study is ever pleasant, and so to Dicky, my landlord, and a summer I spent working for him, which leads back, in a roundabout way, to making friends with Jim.

For as I came to know Dicky, I learned that he had started to construct a bomb shelter in his basement, a project soon overwhelmed by its implications. He had broken through the cement, chunks of which lay around, some shoved back against a wall. He'd dug into the earth as well and most of that had been carried outside; but the hole was irregular, nowhere squared off, and its depth inadequate even as a foxhole. No more than a couple of people could have lain down. And had they covered it with plywood or a tarp, they wouldn't have been able to raise their heads.

It was the summer of 1963, nine months or so after the Cuban Missile Crisis. I'm sure Dicky wasn't alone with such a project though his is one of only two I ever saw. One trouble was his family of six, himself, his wife, and their four children. It would take quite some excavation to contain them all, and they weren't the parent birds to push the least from their nest. That would have been a little rascal still toddling, a boy his two older sisters doted on. No, I'm sure the ludicrous nature of the project dawned on Dicky by the time he had carted away a few bucket-loads of that raw, red Virginia soil. Soil that shocked me. I'd never seen red earth as farmland before and couldn't believe it would nurture anything. Not like the black earth of the Midwest. But corn grew quite well in Virginia too, I would discover after getting used to the red smudges on the rim of these diggings, on my shoes, and on edges of cement chunks stacked beside a basement wall.

Dicky's sizeable family only began the problem. His farm wasn't large, most of it a long pasture that swept up a hill to the east of their house with timber running along it on both sides. His homestead though was the informal center of a hidden neighborhood. Several African American families lived in small houses along the road and on side roads running up draws to the north and south of his pasture and woods. Several of those men worked for Dicky, a few regularly, others when extra work sought them out. What if, under sudden attack, they all came streaming in? Dicky I'm sure would stand up for his family, but I couldn't imagine him setting up a machine gun to mow all the others down and redden that red earth further. I suppose the other side of the equation would also be possible and the gathered neighbors vanquish Dicky and his family as if they had been the Romanovs. Still no shelter that basement could accommodate would handle the victors, whoever they were. Dicky saw the futility of it soon enough. He probably carted out a few more buckets of earth before admitting it to his wife. The best answer, should the alarm come, would certainly be, as others have said, to pour that last fine bourbon and kick back with his feet up on the front porch.

Not that first summer, but a summer later I worked for Dicky. By then I had completed a year of graduate school and had an MA in hand, but if I was to continue for a PhD, I needed summer work. I was young and married and soon enough my wife and I would start our family. We already lived on his grounds, and Dicky made a place for me on his crew of men from the neighborhood.

His chief business, besides managing whatever farm holdings he had, was fence construction. Many landowners, both rural and urban in Albemarle County, wanted to fence their land. There were plenty of white board fences as are familiar in horse country. Split rail fences were another popular option. Then there were standing or woven slats that formed a shield. Dicky oversaw the installation of such fences in Charlottesville and around the county.

He had a standing crew of four: Speedy, Charlie, Brownie, and James. Speedy, the eldest, was not a steady worker. He

171

seemed to show up when he wished. I suppose he was semi-retired. Short, graying, and wiry, his special skill was with the manual posthole digger. It wasn't just that he could plunge its open jaws into the earth, draw them closed by extending those handles wide and extract the red earth of Virginia faster than the rest of us. It was the precision of his cuts, the neat verticality of the sides, the very few bits of crumble at the bottom. When Speedy finished a hole it looked like a bucket in which you could store water.

Charlie was the foreman, though he never ordered Speedy around and more than once deferred to his quiet voice. "You get morning sickness," he asked when my wife became pregnant with our first child. "I always do," he rejoined calmly when I recoiled with surprise and said something like, "of course not." I still don't know whether he was pulling my leg. If so, he didn't betray himself. It seems more likely that he really did share his wife's discomfort and could tutor me in empathy.

I was twenty-five that summer and Charlie significantly older, probably closer to forty than fifty. He oversaw loading the truck, setting up whatever job, and assigned tasks although long habit made most of that unnecessary. Brownie and James, more my peers in both age and on the crew, reminded me of a couple of guys who joined our high school football team a year or two after the Brown Decision. Charlie, a different Charlie, and Shag. The year before they'd been bussed to a high school thirty miles away since our town only provided an eighth grade education for them. Anyone who wished to continue could, but they had to ride that bus every day to the segregated school in another, larger, town. Now, with their hometown school open to them, they joined us. I never got to know them well though we were teammates for three years, and both had to bear the only negative public moment I witnessed.

Our coach, a burly man with curly red hair, had us all indoors on the gym floor before a blackboard. He was diagramming a play. The Xs and Os of offense and defense, the lines from one player to another assigning the blocks, the path the back, possibly Shag, would take on an off-tackle slant and, if everyone did his job, continue for a touchdown. But something was wrong. A defender had been left unblocked. Coach had missed something, and he stood there scratching his head. His back was turned to us as he muttered, more to himself than to us, "There's a n----- in the woodpile somewhere."

It's not as if we were unaware of the expression, but there was an audible gasp and suddenly thickened silence. Coach turned around, puzzled at first, then, scanning our faces, caught on. "I'm sorry," he said. "Never again." And as far as I know, neither he nor any of his assistants uttered another slur. Both Charlie and Shag were formidable players over the next three years, a good deal better than I. Shag went on to play in college.

After the Brown decision, Charlottesville stalled longer on integration than my town had; then for several months in 1959—which was a couple of years after Charlie, Shag, and I had been through school and graduated—the governor ordered its high school closed rather than suffer the inevitable. The courts and the resolve of particular African American families soon corrected that, but it could well have been the end of Brownie and James' schooling. Perhaps they managed no more than eighth grade anyway, since in Charlottesville it was assumed "natural," at least natural enough, as it was also in my hometown, for black youths to put away their books at that point and get on with adult lives. Quite a few white kids dropped out of school at that age too, in both towns. In the small country schools dotted around the midwestern county I came from, boys and girls dressed up smartly for their eighth grade graduation. It might prove their only one.

I expect it would have been for Brownie and James. They were fine workers and could handle any pick, shovel, tractor, hammer, or saw. Over time, we shared much of that, one of us holding a plank or a rail for the other, or steadying a post in its new hole while the other filled in the earth around it and began to tamp it down. We'd all sit in the shade with our lunch boxes. I would listen much more than talk but seek ways to join in. A graduate student, and white, I was the odd man in, sure enough. Once I ran into them downtown, quite by accident, and stopped to greet them, but their lowered glances, deferential manner, and quick readiness to part, more than underscored that.

That accidental crossing of paths reminded me of a time, a few years before, when on Spring Break, I had driven with two college friends, all three of us white, to New Orleans and back. We started from Massachusetts and took with us, on the first leg of our trip, one of the few African Americans in our college. He was from Nashville, right on our way, so we could get him home for the holidays. We started with the weekend and drove all Saturday night to arrive for Sunday dinner. His family welcomed us to their ample table of fried chicken, mashed potatoes with gravy, collard greens—my first exposure to those—and pie; and as we sat with them we learned that his father, the comptroller of Fisk University, had spent his morning bailing students out of jail. And not for the first time. Students were being arrested daily, sitting-in at segregated lunch counters downtown.

A day later, my white pals and I stopped in Oxford, Mississippi, Faulkner country, and as I strolled alone down a sidewalk in the early afternoon, a black man approached from the opposite direction. He was older than I, but as we met he stepped carefully to the side, one foot off the walk, and would not meet my eyes. I was shocked. That had never happened before, not in my hometown and certainly not in Massachusetts, but Brownie and James acted a bit like that when we met in downtown

Charlottesville. I'm sure had I not stopped to greet them, they would have passed on with, at best, a slight wave. During my five years there, it never happened another time.

Nor did it ever occur to me to wonder, much less ask, what my pay was compared to theirs. It's hard for me to imagine that Dicky paid me more than Charlie. But what about Brownie and James? And what did they know, or suspect? That is all hidden now by a half-century of never facing the question.

At work, they had little choice but to accept me; after all, Dicky could hire whomever he liked. The surprise was that they accepted me so readily. I had difficulty understanding their speech at first. Their dialect differed from my own. They, of course, had no trouble understanding me. Charlie, more gregarious than the others, had a gentle teasing streak. That helped. I had jeans and old shirts, good enough work clothes, and I even had work shoes, ankle-high lace-ups of a brownish orange cast with thick, blond rubber soles that showed evidence of previous wear. "Where did you get them boots," Charlie asked. "Don't tell me you wear 'em to class."

No I did not. The uniform of University of Virginia students in my day, still a white male preserve, was a sport coat and tie with chinos or slacks. I had enough of a supply to allow a little variation through the week. But I had done my share of fieldwork. I could drive a pickup and soon showed that I could swing the little Ford tractor around in reverse and line up its mounted auger precisely over the place for the next post hole. I could clean out the hole too, with the two-handled digger, clear away brush with an axe, wield a shovel, a hammer, or saw. I enjoyed driving the tractor. Ours had been much larger John Deeres, and the little Ford was fun; but I made sure not to hog it and to stand at the ready with the manual digger so no deference need be shown. Still, Charlie rather liked getting me up on that tractor. Then when lunch breaks came, we all flopped down in whatever shade, shared the water jug, and I began to share their talk.

In fact they all made allowance for me with considerable grace. Surely I was positioned to brush aside our differences more easily than they. But the muted voices of the two younger men, my peers in age, and for a long time their hesitation with eye contact, suggested that accommodating me was a struggle. At home after work, they no doubt told other stories, and I expect I should be glad not to have heard some of that. All in all though, I took comfort in supposing they could also say, "He's not bad. He's not afraid of work." Or maybe even, "He's competent," which had it come from my uncle, back on our farm, would have been significant praise. On the other hand, I may not have been as competent as I like to think, and at home, they may have pointed that out. They must have had at least a few laughs at my expense.

As aware as I was of trying to join these men, I was inevitably a worker apart, a fact Dicky reinforced by a separate task he gave me. His enterprises included contracting for the installation of private swimming pools. A good number of families scattered around the county went to the effort, and cost, of having an outdoor pool installed at home. Dicky himself had one, and his wife spent a good part of her summer there. As did their four children. My wife and I, who lived in a converted grain shed no more than a couple of hundred yards away, were invited to make free with it as well. That invitation was not extended generally. Certainly not to the men with whom I worked.

I was familiar with pools. Swimming had long been part of my life. Ineffective as a competitive swimmer in college, I had learned to swim well. I became a certified Red Cross Water Safety Instructor, a lifeguard at my hometown pool, and had for one summer directed its instructional program. I'd grown up swimming in that pool, a WPA project of the 1930s, and at a Boy

Scout camp on the Lake of the Ozarks. In a sense, a pool was home ground. My hometown pool had all but closed down one summer, right after the Brown decision, when African Americans showed up at its door. As far as many were concerned, that was one step too far, too soon. But the white kids, too, wanted their pool. The following summer it was wide open, with no interference, not at least of which I was ever aware.

The private pools of Albemarle County were another matter. Once installed, maintenance was necessary. Since they were outdoor pools that meant skimming leaves and other debris off the surface. A rectangular net with a long aluminum handle was left with each pool for that purpose. You could maneuver around and reach anywhere with it. Then you needed to check the ph level of the water and sometimes add chlorine.

This was an awkward job for any man, and for an African American, it could be worse. You couldn't tell whom you might run into at whatever home, in whatever state of aloneness or dress. Therefore, Dicky himself checked up on most of the pools he had contracted. In another year or two, his teenage son would be ready for the job. That summer, however, it fell to me, and I did not resist. In fact, in retrospect, it seems probable that pool maintenance was the chief reason Dicky hired me. That I could fill the rest of my time with his crew was a bonus, but it wasn't as if I was needed there.

Twice a week, I took Dicky's pickup and a half-day or more off from fence building to make the rounds of pools scattered around the county. Crozet, Earlysville, White Hall, Free Union, Ivy, Shadwell, Keene, Covesville, and Keswick were village names I swept through, usually on my way to a nearby farm. No stop took long. I'd skim the leaves, check the chlorine balance, and hop back in the pickup for my next stop. I'd have my lunchbox with a sandwich, an apple or orange, and thermos of milk. I drank coffee by then, but it wasn't the staple it has since become. And whenever I could, before returning to the crew, I'd stop at a small country store for a Fudgsicle.

Fudgsicles hadn't always been my favorite summer treat. All manner of ice cream had been, especially Dairy Queen soft serves with strawberry toppings. But that summer it was Fudgsicles, a chocolate concoction of something-like-ice-cream draped on a stick that I savored all the way down to the stick without, I'd hope, spattering too much on my shirt, not so easy to accomplish driving back roads slowly with the windows down. Then, that stolen pleasure over, I'd haul on home and join the crew, wherever they were, to man a shovel, or a post hole digger, or maneuver the little Ford tractor. The guys always seemed to welcome me back, often with some joshing about where I'd been and what I'd been up to.

Not that I merited any thanks for it, but they were all aware, much more than I, of what I saved them from. What awkwardness, or worse. Which leads to an extension of my story that I couldn't tell Jim those first times we met since it hadn't happened yet. But a few years later, long departed from Charlottesville and in charge of our widely, if thinly distributed literary magazine, I received a submission from Yusef Komunyakaa. He sent several poems, as was the custom, tucked into an envelope with his SASE We hadn't entered the era of digital submissions, so everything came in envelopes, and self-addressed, stamped envelopes came with them. Every week new stories and poems arrived, several dozen of each. Several dozen envelopes, usually several dozen doubled, sometimes tripled and, usually, several poems in each one.

We had not heard of Mr. Komunyakaa, but when his envelope came, I found a poem called "Work." It told of a young man mowing the lawn of a country home and of his resisting the temptation to look at a woman, nude, in a hammock beside the pool, a pitcher of lemonade sweating beside her. The speaker sweats too, and not just from his labor. "I won't look at her," he says and repeats that several times in a narrow poem that in most magazines would take up most of two pages.

It's a garden scene, a fallen garden. Faulkner's ghost hovers nearby. Johnny Mathis, one of the first African American crooners to become popular with white audiences, sings "like a whisper" to the nude, white woman. Komunyakaa revels in the sensuality of the scene. "Bumblebees nudge pale blossoms." The worker breathes in the "Scent of honeysuckle" and "the insinuation of buds/ Tipped with cinnabar." His final image is a "bed/ Of crushed narcissus/ As if gods wrestled there," which they did, the gods of desire resisting those of temptation, while toying with it. One can imagine the woman sharing in the temptation, not least by provoking it. It didn't take long for me to remember my summer with Charlie, Speedy, Brownie, and James and to accept the poem with a silent nod to them. And I was especially glad to learn that Komunyakaa is, indeed, African American.

When I told Jim of our ninth grade teacher fulminating over what would soon befall us—"It's wrong," she had said, "just wrong. I won't stand for it!"—and Carolie's fine response, raising her hand to offer, "Maybe God's changed his mind"—Jim smiled.

"Already an Omni-American," he said, which I suppose he meant only half seriously, but at least she had intuited something of Albert Murray's message long before his book of that name came out. Jim spoke warmly of Murray, who worked closely with Ralph Ellison, and of both as mentors. Omni-America was their subject, with the African American always here and integral to the story, whether whites recognized that or not. Soon I would accept an interview with Ellison, and did so thinking of Jim's admiration for him, while noting especially how Ellison felt sure he had caught whispers of African American music in "The

Waste Land." Whispers he assumed Eliot had picked up as a youth in St. Louis, along our midland river, a river whose main tributary I had grown up beside.

At about the time I met Jim, I was spending a week each summer in Mobile, Alabama, running a workshop for college teachers, and lived alone, through that week, in a house on a golf course outside town. Every morning, I walked down a side road to a clubhouse with a small restaurant. I had bacon, eggs, grits—I really got into the grits, warm with butter melting onto them—toast, and coffee, and read the morning paper. There were rarely any other customers at that hour, but my stay crossed with what must have been break time for grounds keepers. Usually four or five would come in for a late breakfast. They were a mixed group, black and white, and had no trouble sitting together. There they'd be, a distinctly integrated crew of young adults, chatting, laughing in the deepest South. Omni-America was showing itself. I suspect though that it did not extend to their going out together on Saturday nights.

One graduate student I had worked with came from Colorado but had family in Mississippi. As a child she spent summers there, with her grandmother, and for her thesis she wrote of having returned, the summer before, and appealing to her grandmother to visit the African American woman who had cared for her during those distant summers. That woman, now elderly, no longer worked for her grandmother but lived not far away. Her grandmother balked. A visit wasn't possible. But our writer nagged until her grandmother found a way. They would take a walk together, grandmother and granddaughter. They would wear warm-ups, satin pants and jacket, so it was clear they were out for exercise, not to socialize. But they could just happen to walk by the other woman's house. A knock on the door would do no harm, and so a brief visit, one woman standing on her porch, the other two on the road that ran beside it.

When I told of Dicky's bomb shelter and his hypothetical resort to fine bourbon, Jim smiled and said he and his pals had equally extravagant thoughts about those final moments, but they had nothing to do with bourbon. What I learned through our sessions, above all else, was how easy it was for me to not think about race, whereas it was always on Jim's mind. Jim worked hard at being an Omni-American. That was the work of his life. It wasn't mine. In Jim's later years we formed a habit of occasional Sunday brunches after which, often, we'd take a drive in the country. We might stop somewhere for an ice cream cone. Jim would often remark with some surprise that I seemed to know the names of birds and trees, something he had never had the inclination or time for. But on the ground that most mattered between us, Omni-America and how we experienced it, I was always catching up to truths that Jim had long pondered.

All that while, we spoke least of Charlottesville, though it was never distant from our thoughts. One exception was my telling of a Joan Baez concert there. Baez had come on the scene while my wife and I were in college, and this was our first chance to see her. The hall was long and narrow and Ms. Baez her own, lonely accompaniment. In fact the stage was bare, just a backless stool under a light. She took her place on that stool, played her guitar, and sang. One song after another. The long aisle lifted away from the stage so that we looked down on her. She seemed immensely vulnerable. A glass of water stood on a second backless stool beside her. As her concert came to an end, she took the chance of singing "We Shall Overcome." There was that hushed moment between numbers and no announcement of what would come next. Baez just plucked the chord and began. A hush fell over the house. She gestured for us to join in but most held back. A few angry murmurs arose around us. Approval of this anthem was hardly widespread, certainly not in Charlottesville. I would love to say my wife and I were among the first to join her, but we weren't. But a few did, then a few more, and as sides were being drawn, we added our voices. So with help from about a quarter, maybe a third of the house, Joan Baez prevailed with her song. Then she had to make her exit by walking up that long aisle. In fact, she had to be escorted, and I felt I read both worry and defiance in her face as campus security hustled her out.

Through our telling and retelling our stories, Jim and I earned a degree of friendship that endured through the remainder of his days. It would be presumptuous for me to assume it was more than it was, which at best, perhaps, amounted to a courtesy Jim extended almost as if, indeed, we were friends. At courtesy, civility, and negotiating the right distance, Jim was more subtle than my former student's grandmother. In any case we put our issue together, collaborated another time or two, and kept on seeing each other until he died. When the issue Jim guest-edited appeared in 1985, it happened to coincide with the centennial of *Huckleberry Finn*. I commissioned a woodcut for our cover. The artist, one of our graduate students, made a clever one of Huck sitting on a dock with a pipe in his mouth, reading a book. There's a smile. Let him be reading our magazine. Meanwhile a steamboat passes by, one of those old paddlewheelers emblematic of the era. Of course Jim, Huck's Jim, isn't in the picture, and it never occurred to me to make that suggestion.

A Certain Arc

But I wanted to describe the trajectory of a baseball, the air, the rustling air, the space—the hole the ball makes against the background, its shape and how it has warped by the time it reaches me. . . .
—Mickey Mantle, as rendered by Nathalie Léger

A couple of years ago my wife and I reread *Moby-Dick*, which led her to *Omoo, Typee, Redburn,* and *Pierre*, which, by the way, she recommends unequally. It led also to her observing, shortly before Christmas, how she thought she needed a few books by women. I took the hint and came up with four with which I stuffed her stocking. Thus, about a month later, she read the passage above aloud, over coffee, at our kitchen table. It's from the third of the four books she received. By that time I'd heard fragmentary reports on each of the first two. But this was different. The passage comes about half way through a late section of the book, which she read with rising fervor. By the time she hit the arc of a baseball, I knew I too would be reading Nathalie Léger's *Suite for Barbara Loden,* (France 2012, Dorothy Project 2016 in the English translation of Natasha Lehrer and Cécile Menon). Nor would I have to wait long for it comes quite near the end of the book, a small book, barely one hundred twenty-three pages, which Rebecca passed on to me within the hour.

Assigned an entry on Loden for a French encyclopedia of film, Léger saw Loden's film, *Wanda,* and soon found herself immersed in a story beyond her grasp, a story of Wanda, the woman whose story *Wanda* had been based upon, of Loden, of Léger's mother, and of Léger herself. Eventually she traveled to the States to meet Loden's sons and Elia Kazan, Loden's husband at the time of her death in 1980, to travel around Connecticut and northeastern Pennsylvania where *Wanda* was shot, read Kate Chopin's *The Awakening,* which was to be Loden's next project, and interview several other people, including Frederick Wiseman, who tipped her off to Mantle. Mantle, he said, knew Loden when she was a Copacabana dancer.

The image of the ball in flight, of the "hole" it makes in air, turns out to be a purposeful replay of the image with which *Suite for Barbara Loden,* called a novel but inexactly that, begins: "a woman etched against the darkness. . . . a tiny white figure, barely more than a dot against the dark expanse," and so a hole in air, a striking image of both presence and absence, an image touched on several times later. Wiseman's tip not only encourages Léger to touch all the bases she can, but gives her, or secures for her, or amplifies an image she may already have had. Wiseman offers another tip as well. Loden has proved elusive, leaving Léger with numerous questions unlikely to be resolved. "What do you do when you can't find answers," she asks Wiseman, an as-far-as-we-know scrupulous documentarian. "Make it up," he replied, "all you have to do is make it up." Here was a more elegant way with that question than the labored, unsmiling, defensive ones I have had occasion recently to read and overhear. I smiled, read on, and imagined Léger connecting with her image and knocking it right out of the park. Nor was I surprised to find, a little farther on, baseball playing on a telly in a tavern and Léger asking a man at the bar, "how long do you have to train to be able to hit such a small ball with a stick."

Léger's term is "autofiction," a blend no longer unfamiliar, if it ever was, of fact, personal history, memory, and story; her version in *Suite* composed of one hundred fifteen (unnumbered) paragraphs, some long, some short, separated by white space. To read *Suite* is to read a flow, or to read the stepping-stones across a larger, more subtle flow where the footing is slippery. The Mantle paragraph, the one-hundred-fifth (109-115), is the longest of the book. The *New Yorker* reviewer finds it the book's one blemish, riding, as he sees it, on the cliché of the inarticulate jock. Another, finding in it a "perfected Mantle," can only ascribe that to Léger's "slight of hand." A third prints much of it as a sidebar, letting that stand as a de facto review of the book.

The possible "slight of hand" had struck both of us right off and has everything to do with why Rebecca read me the passage to begin with. For the most part it is given as indirect discourse, perhaps a summary of what Mantle told Léger, perhaps her recreation of that as best she could, like Capote in his motel room at night after his interviews, having carried no recorder or even notebook along, or perhaps an idealization of what she took Mantle to have intended. Or of what she wanted him to say. But a brief direct quotation begins the interview, several lines given as such, and these set Léger off. She and Mantle meet, improbably, at the Houdini Museum in Scranton, Pennsylvania, to which Mantle made occasional visits. He was interested in Houdini's "crazy hope of making contact with his mother who died in 1913—around the same time, I think, that your Proust was doing the same thing with his writing, isn't that right?"

Whoa, Mantle, Houdini, spiritualism, writing, and Proust; isn't that something? "You never know who the other person will turn out to be," the late Jim McPherson said more than once on a Sunday afternoon drive after brunch at the Motley Cow, or the Hamburg Inn, or occasionally McDonald's, which Jim would call "going to church." He spoke of men he had met as a railroad porter when he was young, of who other porters turned out to be, the backgrounds and education they had. There had been surprises, just as Jim, over time, surprised many. Jim smiled at all that just as he may well have smiled at our surprise, my surprise, Nathalie Léger's surprise that Mantle would know of Proust.

Mantle had been urged to write his memoirs, and he wanted to write them himself. To employ a ghost would have been "taking the bat out of his hands." Moreover, he wasn't satisfied to gossip about rivalry, camaraderie, feuds, and team travels, or the women he found at the Copacabana and elsewhere, or who found him. He wanted to write what he especially and all but uniquely knew. And so the passage with which I began, which continues, "[the ball's] exact line when it takes off again, that I conceive in my mind a millisecond before I hit it, afterward I don't look at it any longer, I've already gone, I'm not looking at it but I keep an eye on it, that's something else—that's what I wanted to tell." Not to look at it but to "keep an eye on it," that is something else. Maybe Léger was mesmerized by Mantle's account and wanted to write it as well as she could.

Writing it well had been Mantle's problem. He soon discovered the seemingly infinite possibilities of sentences, of which words and where they could be placed, the subtlety of that, comparable to his manager, Casey Stengel, signaling him to inch over a little, left or right, out there in centerfield. He felt a little lost on this vastly different landscape where he could no longer trust his instincts. So he read for help. That too is something else. He didn't call for help, he read Hemingway and Melville and, because a son's girlfriend studied French at NYU, he was led "to read a bit of Proust—just a bit—but I still couldn't describe the trajectory of a baseball, no more than I could describe Barbara Loden."

Several issues dance now at my fingers' tips. One is that Mantle spoke as an expert, there being very few men in the world, and I guess they would be men, whom we could imagine having as refined a sense of that experience with a speeding hardball as he. We readers may find it comforting to believe that intellect and athletic prowess are mutually exclusive, but every now and then, listening to an interview, we trip over that cliché when surprised by how articulate an athlete turns out to be; that is, by who he, or she, really is, at some moments anyway. And I am reminded of the time when I was absorbed in creating sequences of writing assignments, each prompt emerging from the last, toward an unfolding investigation of a single subject— an anemometer, a rose window, the anatomy of a fish—all based on the supposition that as the writer learned more and more about her subject—really got into it and came within range of imagining herself a specialist—she would find more exact and articulate explications of it, just as Mantle might through his numerous solo encounters with a hardball. Nor have I, as an academic, ever been expected to write outside my field, even if "field" in my case was often a little hard to name. For we all know the term comes from somewhere and along with it the expectation that as we tend our field, and attend to it, we will refine our work. That if you put a microphone in my face and ask me to hold forth on microeconomics, sub-atomic particles, the politics of southeast Asia, or a baseball spinning toward me at nearly 100 mph, I would do well to sound like a dumb jock. And when Mantle says, "around the same time, I think, that your Proust was doing the same thing with his writing," his suddenly hesitant speech was a tactful sign of knowing his thoughts raced toward an outfield wall and he sensed its warning track.

One of my greatest pleasures in reading has always been to discover who someone turns out to be, Ishmael swaying in the rigging and waxing philosophically of the sea, its creatures, and its depths. Nearly anyone in Shakespeare, say quick-witted Viola who fends off the misguided advances of Olivia while she waits for a certain Duke to learn who they both really are. Or Huck, of whom you wouldn't have heard without you had read a book by the name of *The Adventures of Tom Sawyer*, but that ain't no matter now 'cause you'll learn a good deal more soon enough, including glimpses of his lyrical heart:

> You see the mist curl up off the water, and the east reddens up, and the river, and you make out a log cabin in the edge of the woods, away on the bank on t'other side of the river, being a wood-yard, likely, and piled by them cheats so you can throw a dog through it any-wheres; then the nice breeze springs up . . . and next you've got the full day, and everything smiling in the sun, and the song-birds just going it!

Where do these characters come from? How do they transcend our expectations? There are many answers, all partial, but one thing I suspect is common: their authors' belief in them, in their possibility. When Marilynne Robinson replied to Rebecca's greeting that morning with "Oh, I'm enjoying the company of my narrator," she was offering confirmation. Her narrator would have been Reverend John of *Gilead,* and as you get to know him, through the long letter he writes his son, you don't find it hard at all to believe in his extended conversations with Marilynne over coffee at her kitchen table. All she had to do was make him up.

Loden died in 1980, Mantle in 1995. Léger's book came out seventeen years after Mantle's death. Léger herself was born in 1960. This must have been an early assignment, one she might not have accepted after she became her accomplished self. She has published another novel as well as *Suite,* has curated exhibitions on Beckett and Barthes, and is the Executive Director of IMEC *(Institut mémoires de l'édition contemporaine)*, an institution that archives the publishing industry in France. I can well imagine an aging Mantle taking time to chat with a bright woman in her early thirties when she was just getting her start. That's not hard to imagine at all. Léger creates a tender moment that prompts Mantle's extended discourse:

> He is old. Once upon a time he had red hair. He used to be a womanizer. Getting up to go to the drinks machine he rises too quickly and loses his balance. Now, standing there talking to me, small and compact, a can of Sprite in one hand, while he steadies himself against the drinks machine with the other, he appears to be concentrating on some longstanding pain.

Thus Mantle rises to the occasion of speaking about what he wanted to write, the perplexing hope of that, and of learning how hard it would be. An old man at this point, though only in his early sixties, he is caught off balance, something he rarely experienced in the field, in his field anyway, but not on this other one adjacent to it that he came, it seems, to care for. So as if to catch his arm and steady him, Léger does just that. Perhaps she too was subject to some longstanding pain; several moments in the text suggest as much. Though an early assignment led her to Mantle, apparently it took her years to find her way to writing it right.

Suite, I'll suppose, nagged at Léger a long while. There are hints she still lived with her mother when she took it on since her mother, like her editor, reminds her it's only a page or two; why not get on with it and then to something else? The answer probably lies in the undercurrent swirling beneath our stepping-stones that is really the main stream of the book, which is not Mantle but more or less his opposite. The protagonist of *Wanda* is a woman who takes up with a man who can only bring trouble but goes along with him, less out of positive attraction than out of her lack of will to resist. Eventually he drags her into an attempted bank robbery as the getaway driver. They go separately. She makes a wrong turn—passive aggression, perhaps—and arrives late. Her partner has been shot dead. Arrested, she goes on trial, is convicted, and sentenced to twenty years. At her sentencing, she thanks the judge for at long last solving her life. Wanda's willingness to go along with the robber and then with the judge, her thankfulness in the end for having her life resolved, drew Loden and then Léger to her story.

Clearly the story spoke to Loden who not only filmed it but played the part. "Barbara Loden *is* Wanda, as they say in the movies," Léger affirms right off. Her story speaks to Léger's mother, who after her divorce found herself wandering around the largest mall in France, feeling like a tiny figure, perhaps in white, etched against a dark expanse. For a long time she had mostly gone along with. Now she was free if a little lost. Léger mentions but never elaborates on a comparable story of her own, but it too swirls in those depths. For that matter, who hasn't sometimes, perhaps often, found it easier to go along with than to resist?

I knew a woman once who felt an attraction to pornography. I knew her well. We have a son and daughter to show for it, both grown now and parents themselves. We were young parents together and married for a bunch of years. Once we drove to Detroit to see *The Devil in Miss Jones*. We didn't see *Deep Throat*, but it was that era. Years later, in another town, we both read *9 ½ Weeks* then went to see the film though I remember feeling a little abashed to watch, with her, Mickey Rourke and Kim Basinger act out various forms of psychic and physical bondage. Later I asked her what she found compelling. "It takes it all out of your hands," she replied, "you don't have to decide anything." In our daily lives, she did carry, insisted upon, and certainly felt responsible for a considerable burden of decision, and for worrying about it. "Someone around here should get points for worrying," she complained with a forced smile. As for me,

I wasn't overly shy but I wasn't exactly a take-charge guy. I believed every word she said.

For most of us it is far easier to believe in characters we dream up than to believe in ourselves. Or to put that differently, it is easier to go along with who others take us to be than to insist on being who we want to believe we are. That women are especially prone to this particular captivity I am perfectly willing to imagine, but I don't find it foreign to myself.

So let's return to Mantle's story as written by Léger, quite possibly with considerable "slight of hand." The *New Yorker* reviewer was right to point it out, but less as a blemish than as the feature that stands apart. Perhaps it is ballast, a kind of counterweight to the rest of this troubled book. I find I believe in Léger and in her Mickey Mantle. I believe in the confidence she found, born of urgencies I do not know, to give him her arm at the drink machine and help him stand as she found he wished to stand. But her book is about Loden, and *Wanda,* and the woman's story *Wanda* was based upon; it is about the silent acquiescence of women who endure their pain rather than believing they might fend if off, even with a stick.

Their pain is the point. If we were to anthropomorphize a ball, we could imagine its pain after Mantle gives it a whack. And the whacked ball as woman is what this book is about, especially the enigma she becomes as an emblem of endurance. In one, shall I say striking example, Kazan writes a novel, *The Arrangement,* that however a blend as autofiction, is presumed to portray much of Loden's life. "I thought it was about me," she says. And she felt betrayed. Then she was the more betrayed when Faye Dunaway got the lead role when Kazan adapted his novel to film. Dunaway had been Loden's understudy in her one stage triumph, her lead in Arthur Miller's *After the Fall,* understood by nearly everyone as based on Miller's life with Marilyn Monroe. Kazan had argued for Loden then, had "insisted on her being cast." In that case, too, Loden identified with the part. But now in filming his own book, largely about Loden, Kazan made Loden's former understudy "more than her very self."

Léger's story is Loden but also Wanda in whom Loden saw herself; which means it is also the woman Loden read about who was the basis for Wanda's story. It is Monroe, or more precisely the character in Miller's play based on Monroe whom Loden plays on Broadway. Loden stands at the head of a line of receding stand-ins for herself, or at its base, like the turtle beneath all turtles, the one on which her world rests. Then there is Léger who sees in Loden much of what Loden saw in all the others. Though not a triumphant actor, Loden had her moment in *Wanda,* where she caught the eye of Marguerite Duras, for one, Isabelle Huppert for another. Interviewing Huppert about the movie, Léger hears her say, "The more one is absent, the greater chance one has of being present in front of the camera." Elusiveness is the greater presence. Writing in search of Loden, Léger comes to place herself at the end of that line, as elusive to herself as any of the others; and she writes of Mantle.

Mantle is Loden's opposite: overt, clear-lined, certain— except for how to write himself. How better for a woman writer to absent herself than by portraying a famous male athlete? He is the massive background against which we lose her, like a ball hit so high and far it transcends the park, the hole in air through which she escapes. And she is all the more present for it.

They have a connection, those two, the surprise of Proust, but even more of Mantle's desire not to portray himself directly with all the obvious accouterments of celebrity, but as a batsman unusually able to keep his eye on the ball and hit it so convincingly that we take our eyes off him and follow the ball instead as it diminishes in our sight. We keep our eye on him, but we follow the ball, especially as readers ready for the disappearing act of a good story. "What does the truth look like?" asks Jean-Luc Godard in Léger's epigraph. "It's between appearing and disappearing," he says in reply to himself.

Compared to the mystery of the woman's mostly silent, inarticulate feeling, Mantle, Léger finds, can be understood. This runs us right up against another cultural cliché, not of the inarticulate jock, but the yang and yin of male and female: that man is outward and obvious, woman inward and subtle. Then the projection of that onto parallel configurations: the subjected know their oppressors better than oppressors know their subjects, even in some hands to the division of East and West. Thus the more Loden and Wanda are inarticulate and inarticulable, the more profound we find them; and with Mantle, the reverse. He can be understood, his profundity expressed. Léger understands him. She also finds she cannot help but make him sympathetic in ways she would not have guessed. That commentators spark to the passage only proves her point. Even if it does come quite late in the book, Léger has found her hook.

Coda

When I first sent out poems a few decades ago and had not published any, one set was rejected by a woman editor who found their sensibility "oddly feminine." Perhaps I should have sent them right back out under the name Denise. Instead I let her stump me for several years. When I did publish poems finally, an early instance was a chapbook of four that seems so incidental I've never included it on my CV. A friend taking a letterpress-printing course needed work for her final project. Poems would be better than prose: fewer words per page and, given the irregularity of lines, an opportunity for design. Of course I had some, typed out and shoved into a drawer. I gave her a handful, she chose four, prefaced them with a print of her own and put out a little book. I called it *A Hole in Air* and still have several copies somewhere between appearing and disappearing on my highest shelf.

Acknowledgements

Most of these essays were published before, in whole or in part, and several have been revised since their first publications, which were:

"Hometown" as "American Gothic," in *A Place of Sense*, edited by Michael Martone, University of Iowa Press (1988), 66-95.

"In an Innertube, on the Amazon," *Michigan Quarterly Review* (Summer 1990), 372-392.

"Someone Is Leaving: A Ghost Story," *Michigan Quarterly Review* (Spring 1996), 337-357. Special thanks to my daughter, Jenny Bogoni, for allowing her letter home to end my story.

Portions of "At the Fair" in *The Chariton Review* (Fall 2008), 33-39, and *The Iowa Review* 39.1 (2009), 190-195.

Thanks also to Christine Deavel for permission to reproduce her poem in this essay.

"Charlottesville," *The Iowa Review* 48.3 (2018/19): 39-49.

"A Certain Arc," *Fourth Genre* 19. 2 (Fall 2017): 129-137.

Special thanks to my imaginative and generous-minded editors: Michael Martone; Larry Goldstein; Jim Barnes; Kate Conlow, Lynne Nugent, and Harry Stecopoulos; Laura Julier; and now in this collected presentation, Steve Semken and Harley McIlrath. I am especially grateful for the interest they have shown, and the care they have taken with my manuscript.

David Hamilton was a member of the English Department at the University of Iowa for thirty-seven years, teaching both literature and writing courses. Through most of those years, too, he edited *The Iowa Review*. His earlier books are *Deep River: A Memoir of a Missouri Farm*, and *Ossabaw* and *The Least Hinge*, a volume and chapbook of poems.

The Ice Cube Press began publishing in 1991 to focus on how to live with the natural world and to better understand how people can best live together in the communities they share and inhabit. Using the literary arts to explore life and experiences in the heartland of the United States we have been recognized by a number of well-known writers including: Gary Snyder, Gene Logsdon, Wes Jackson, Patricia Hampl, Greg Brown, Jim Harrison, Annie Dillard, Ken Burns, Roz Chast, Jane Hamilton, Daniel Menaker, Kathleen Norris, Janisse Ray, Craig Lesley, Alison Deming, Harriet Lerner, Richard Lynn Stegner, Richard Rhodes, Michael Pollan, David Abram, David Orr, and Barry Lopez. We've published a number of well-known authors including: Mary Swander, Jim Heynen, Mary Pipher, Bill Holm, Connie Mutel, John T. Price, Carol Bly, Marvin Bell, Debra Marquart, Ted Kooser, Stephanie Mills, Bill McKibben, Craig Lesley, Elizabeth McCracken, Derrick Jensen, Dean Bakopoulos, Rick Bass, Linda Hogan, Pam Houston, and Paul Gruchow. Check out Ice Cube Press books on our web site, join our email list, Facebook group, or follow us on Twitter. Visit booksellers, museum shops, or any place you can find good books and support true honest to goodness independent publishing projects so you can discover why we continue striving to "hear the other side."

Ice Cube Press, LLC (Est. 1991)
North Liberty, Iowa, Midwest, USA
steve@icecubepress.com
twitter @icecubepress
www.icecubepress.com

to Fenna Marie and
your brave wonderful life
from where you've come and how it's
all stretched out in an arc before you
your legacy is alive and well and burning bright